House of Nika's Art Therapy

Colour yourself calm.

by Anika Moore

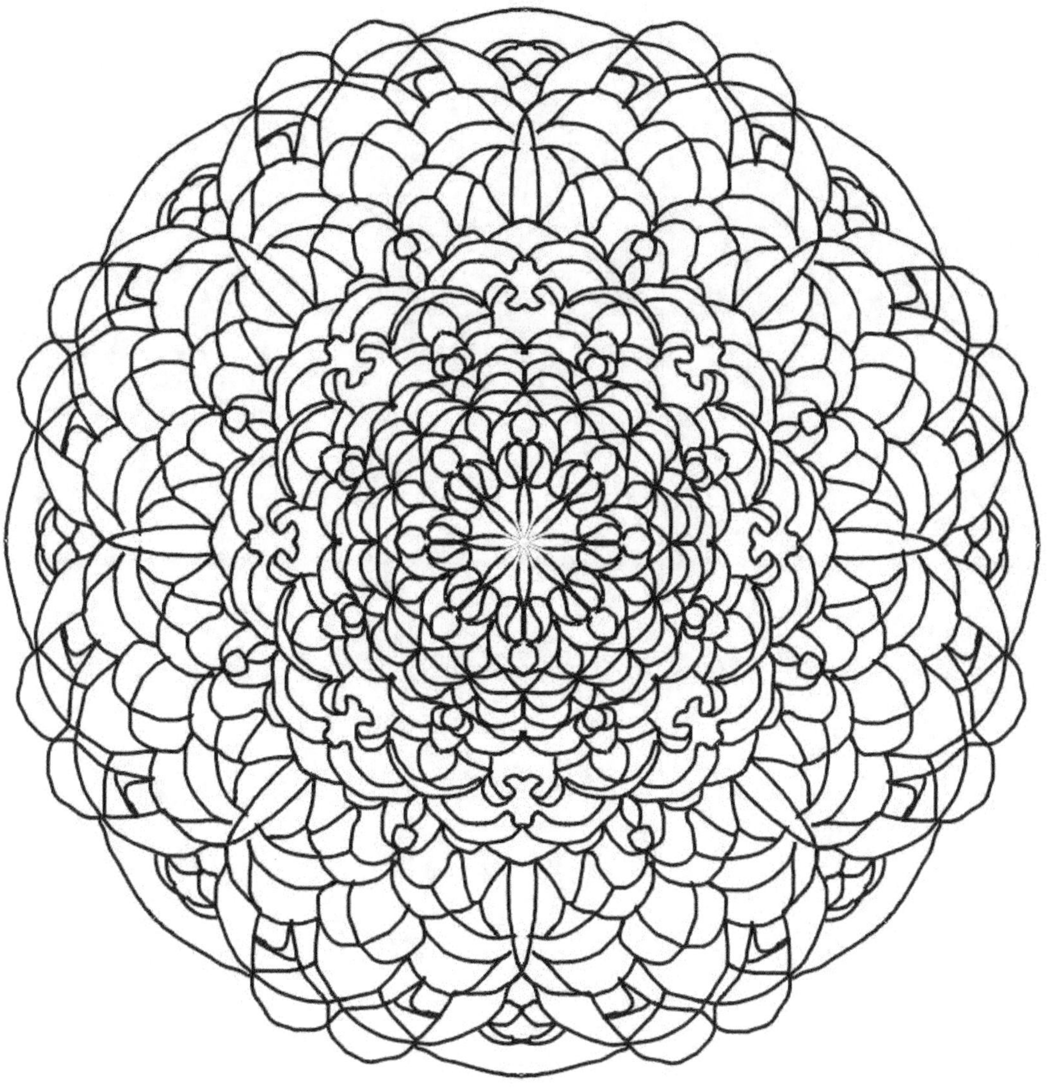

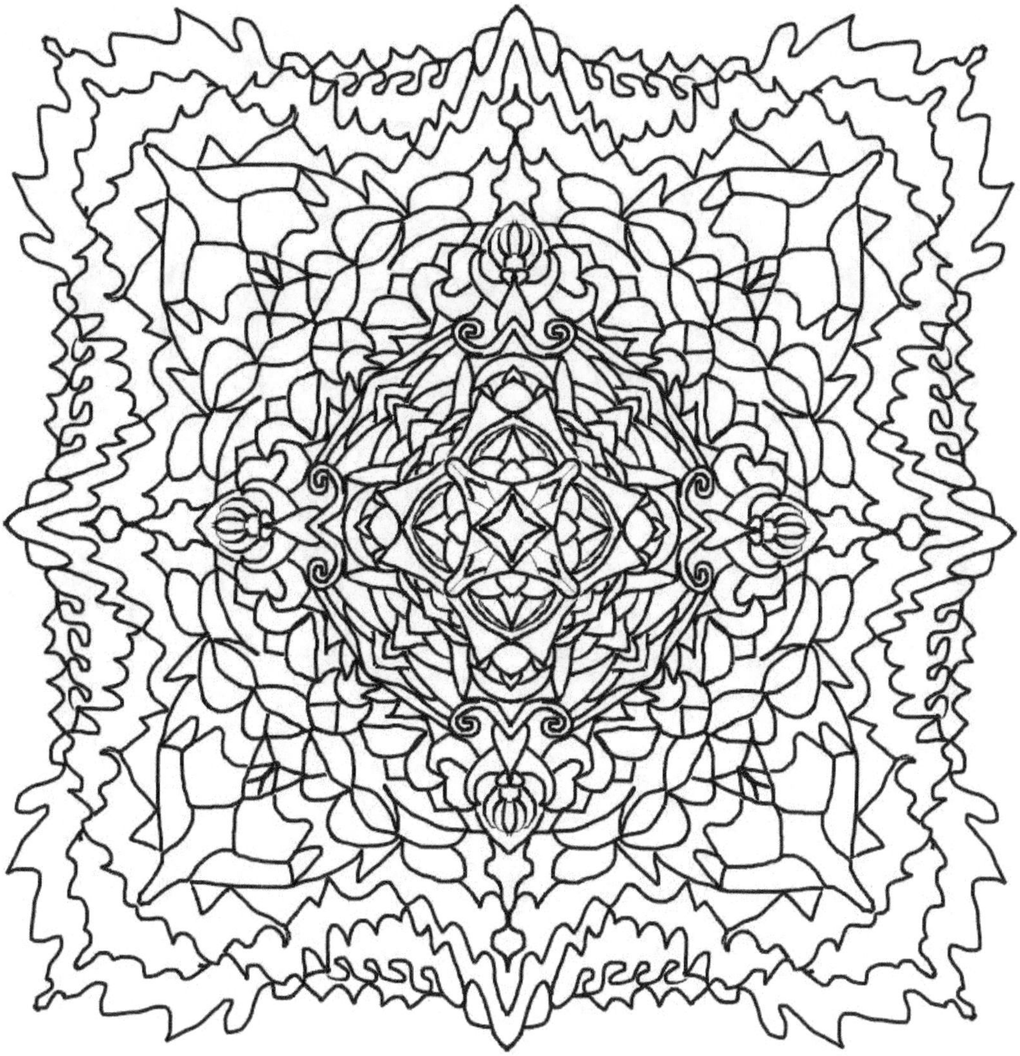

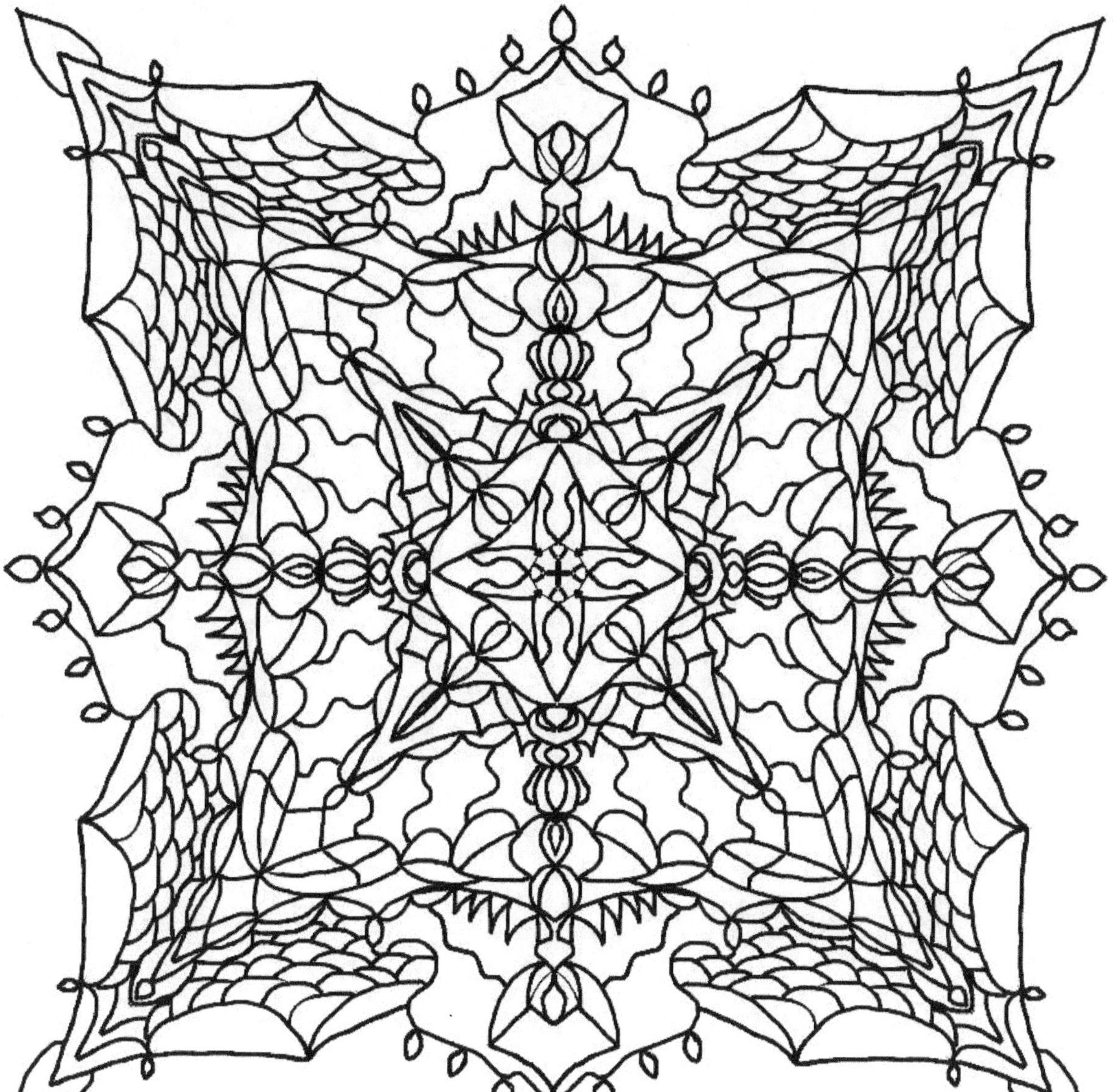

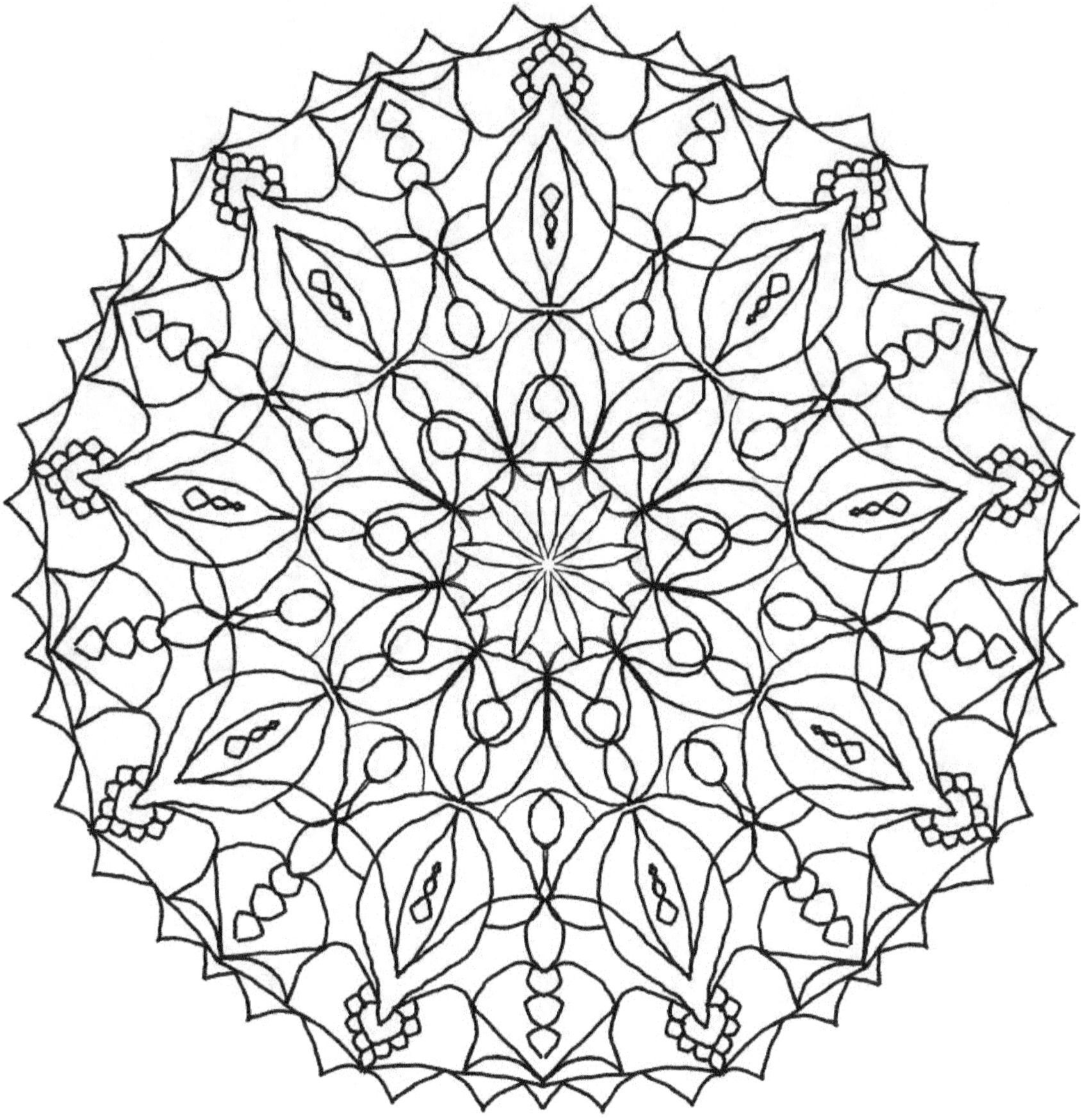

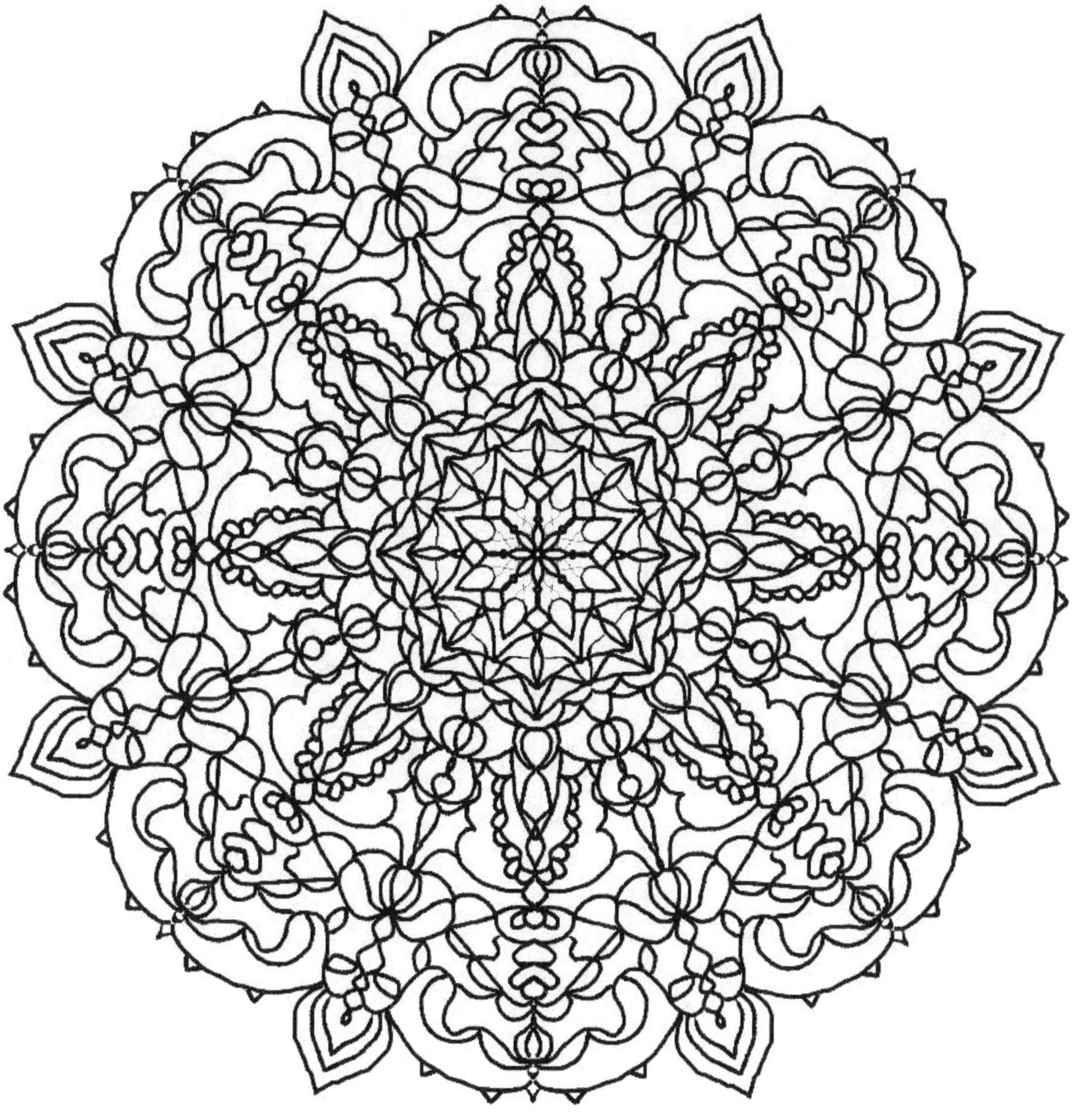

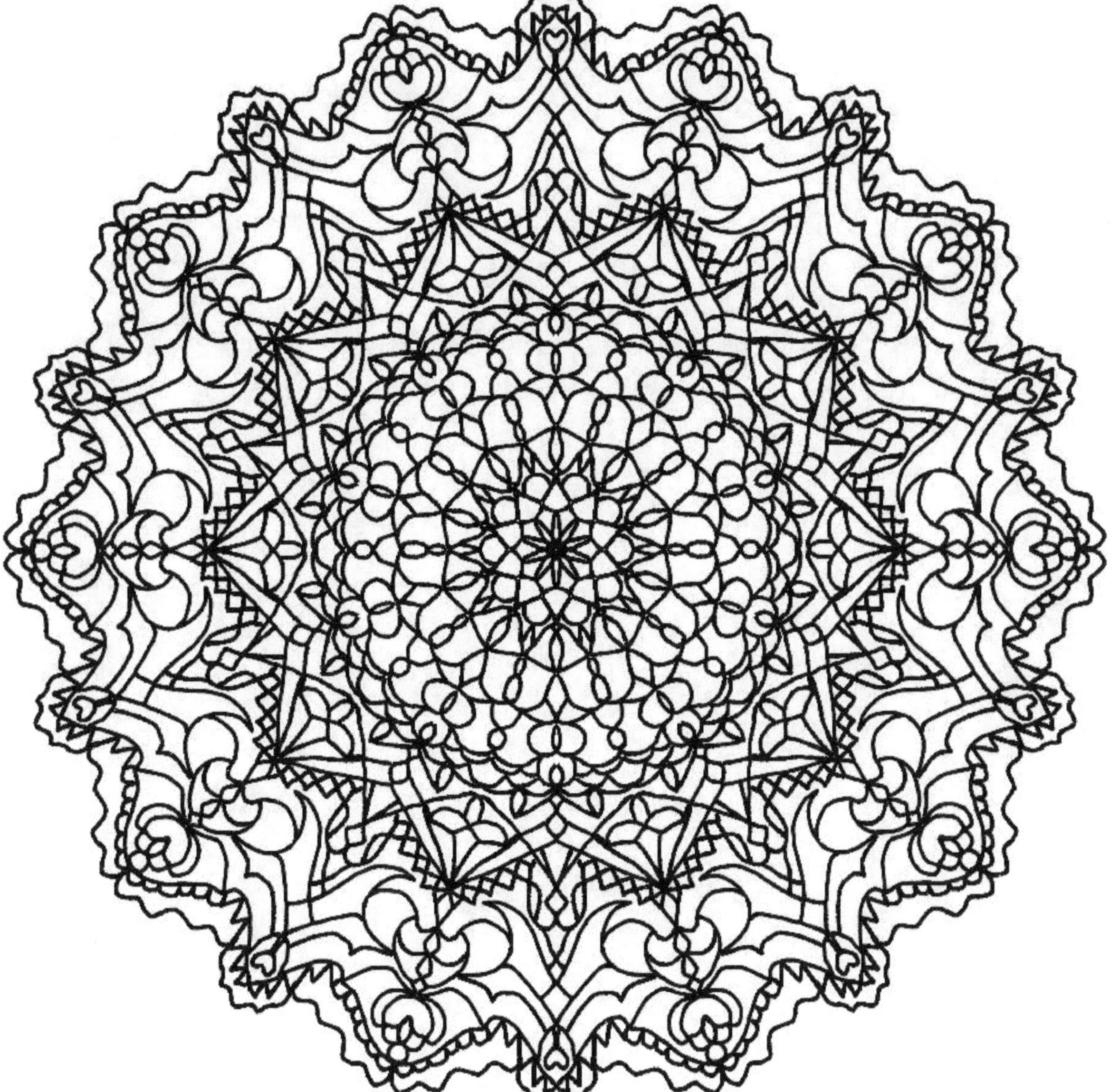

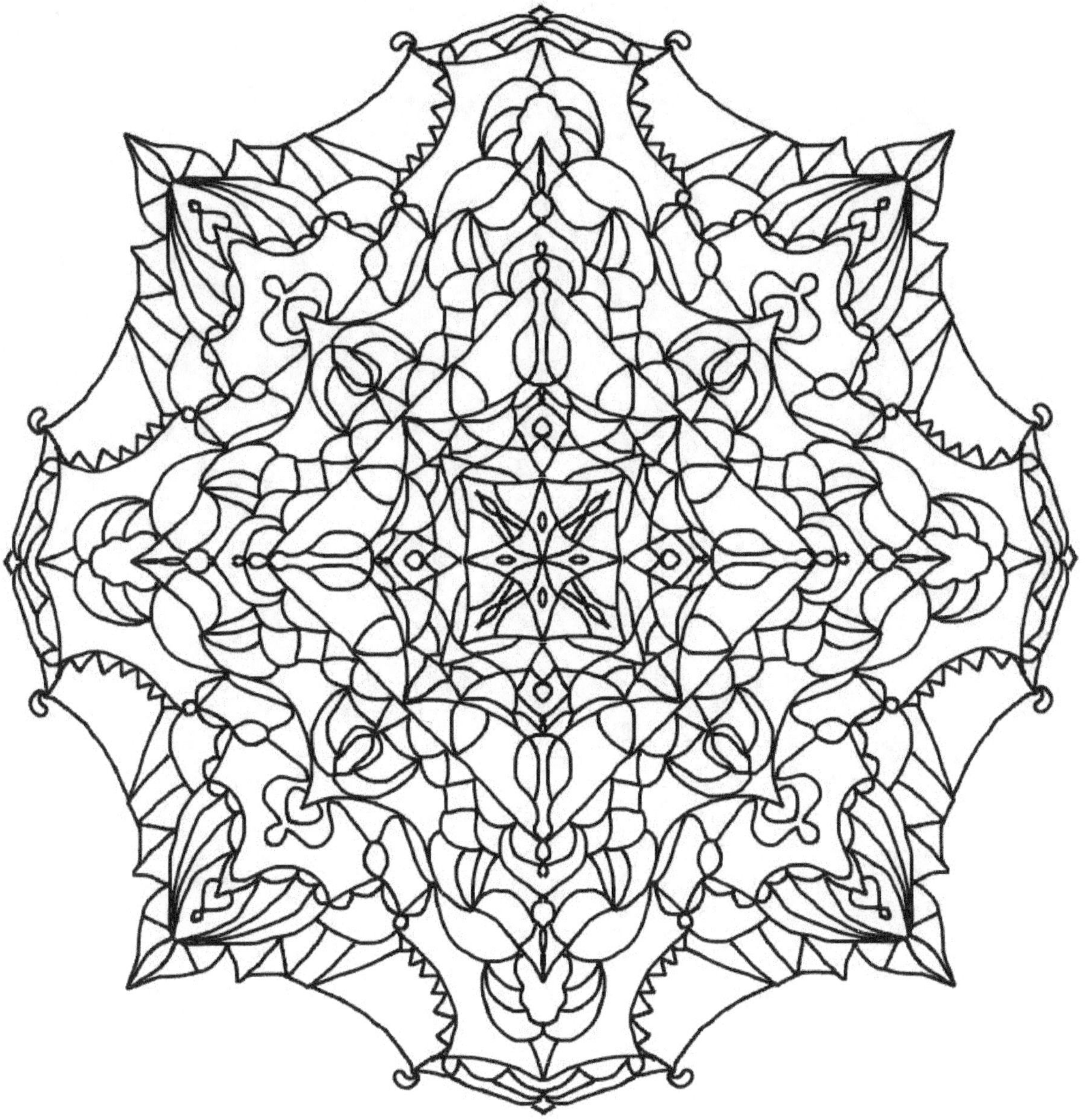

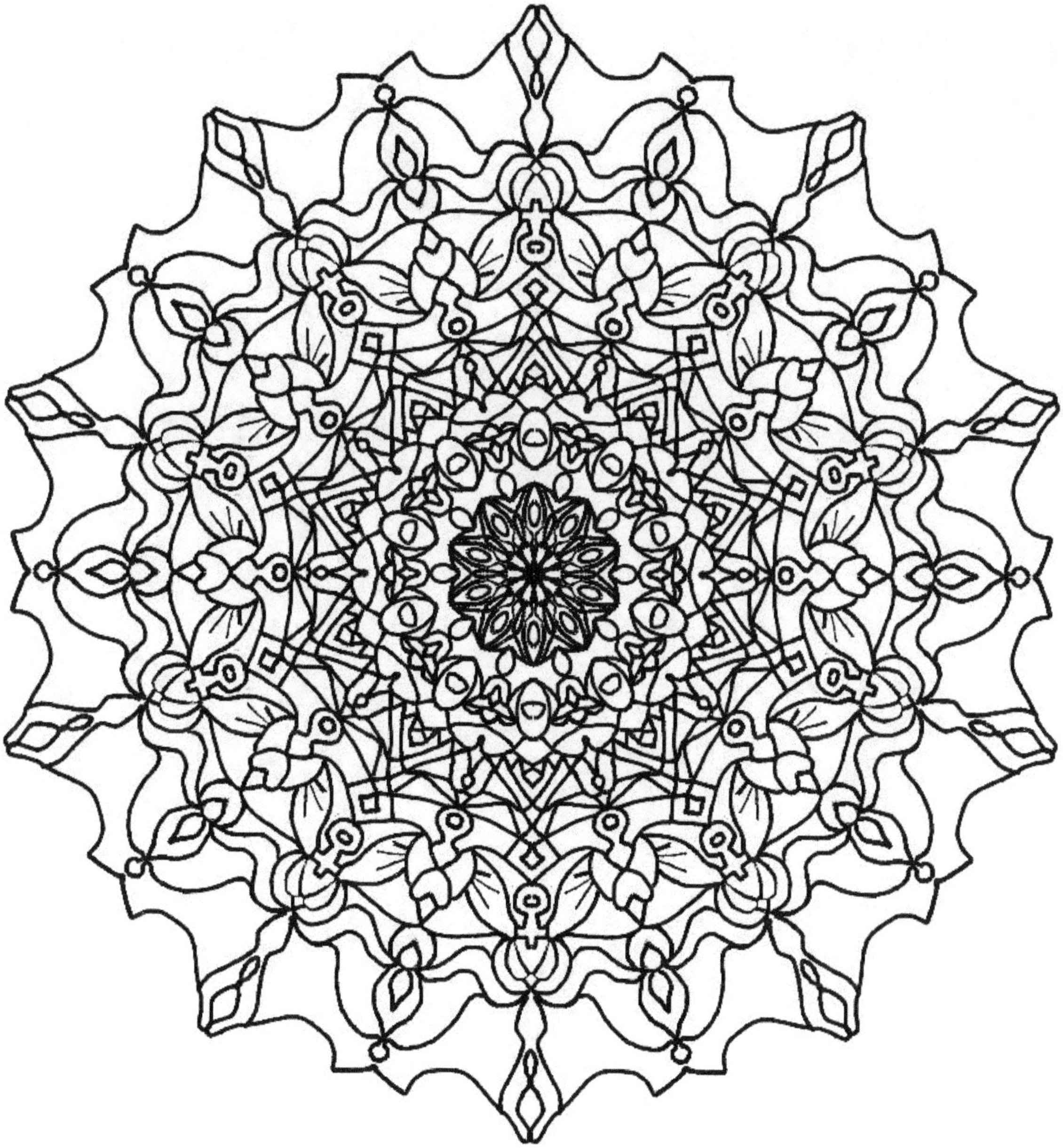

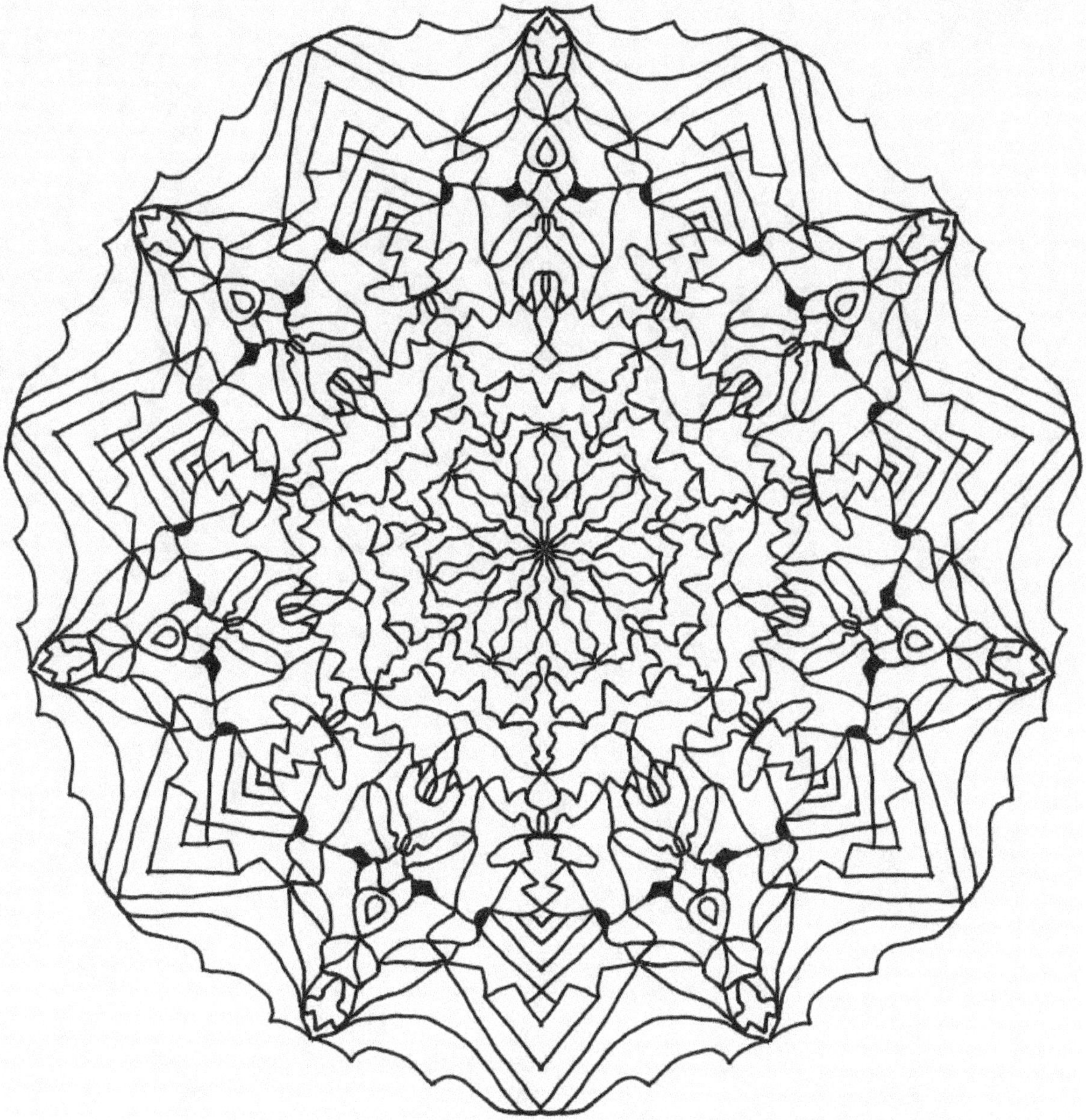

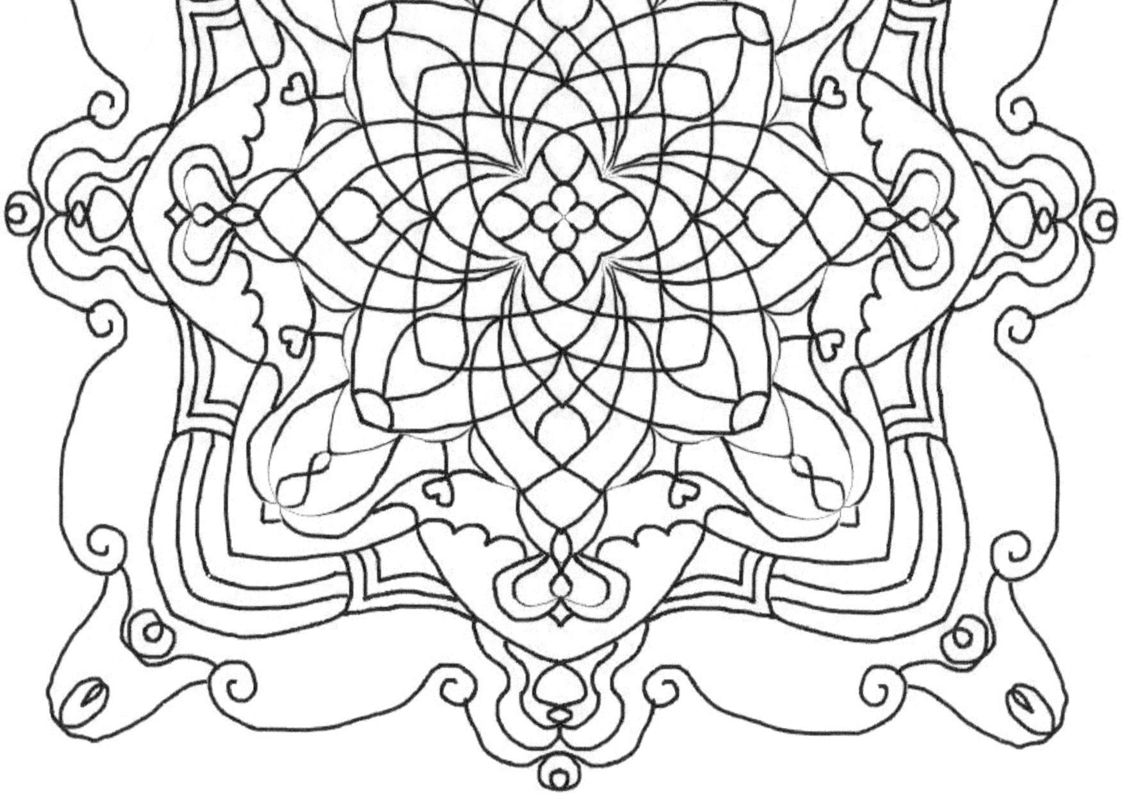

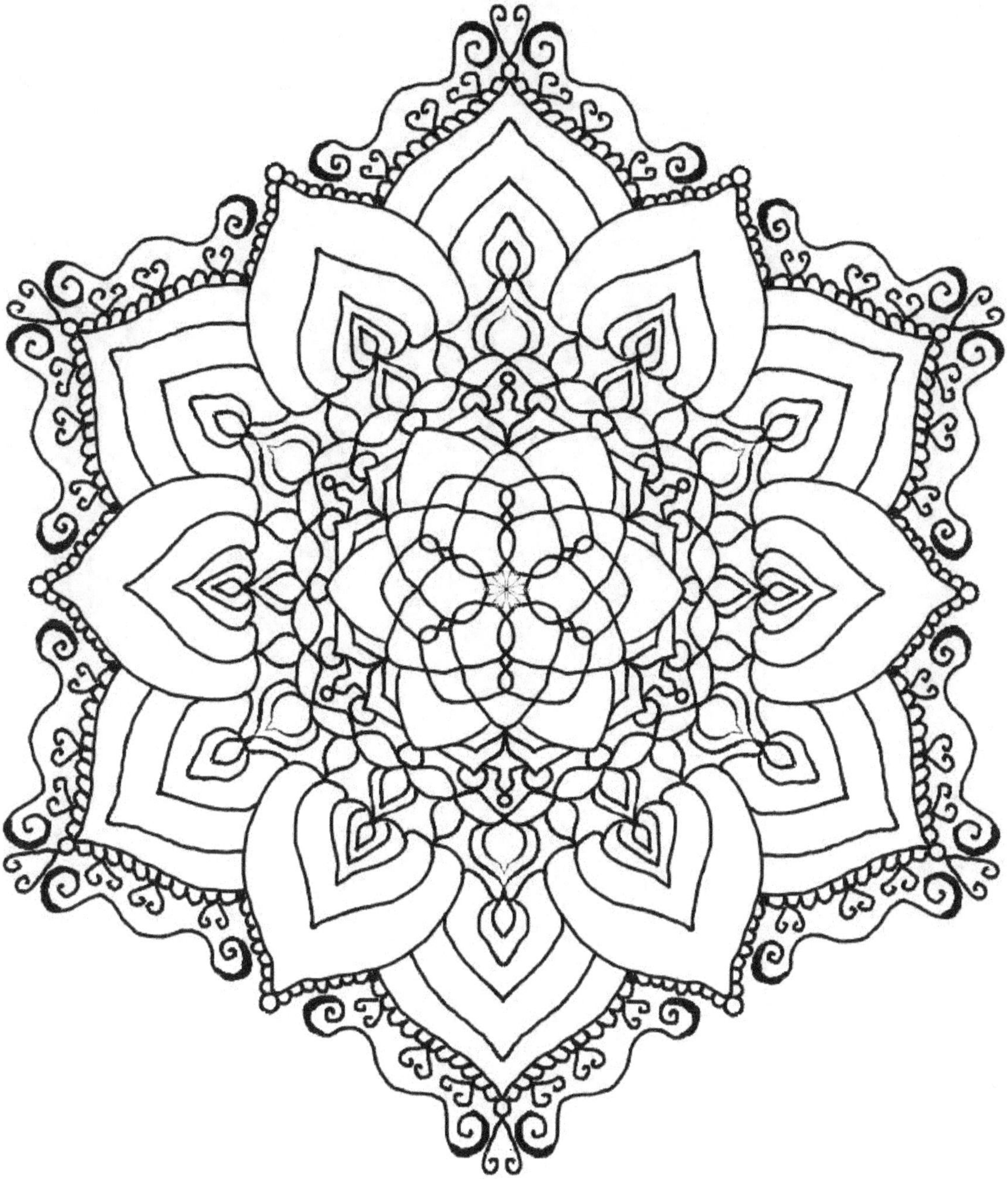

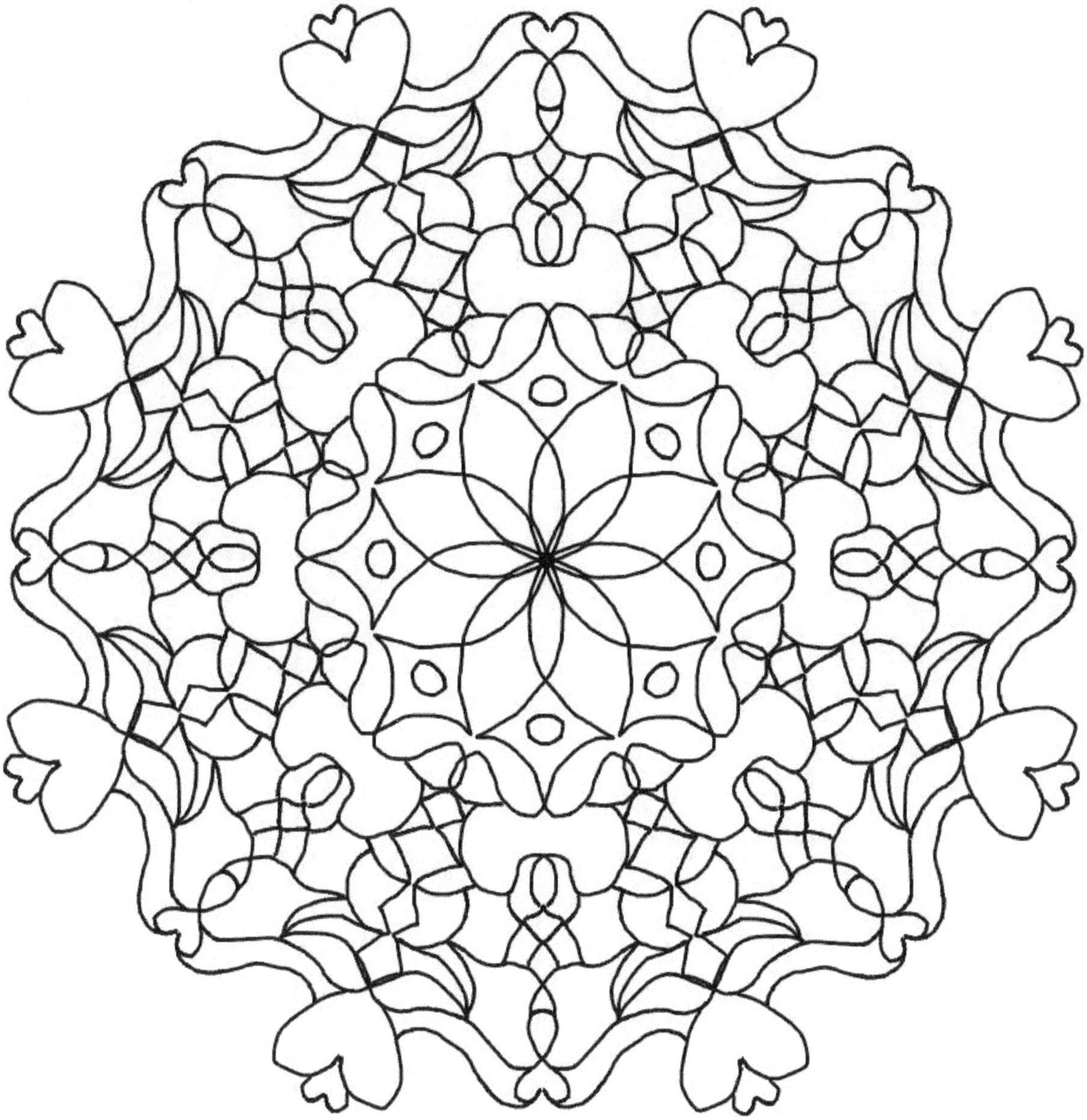

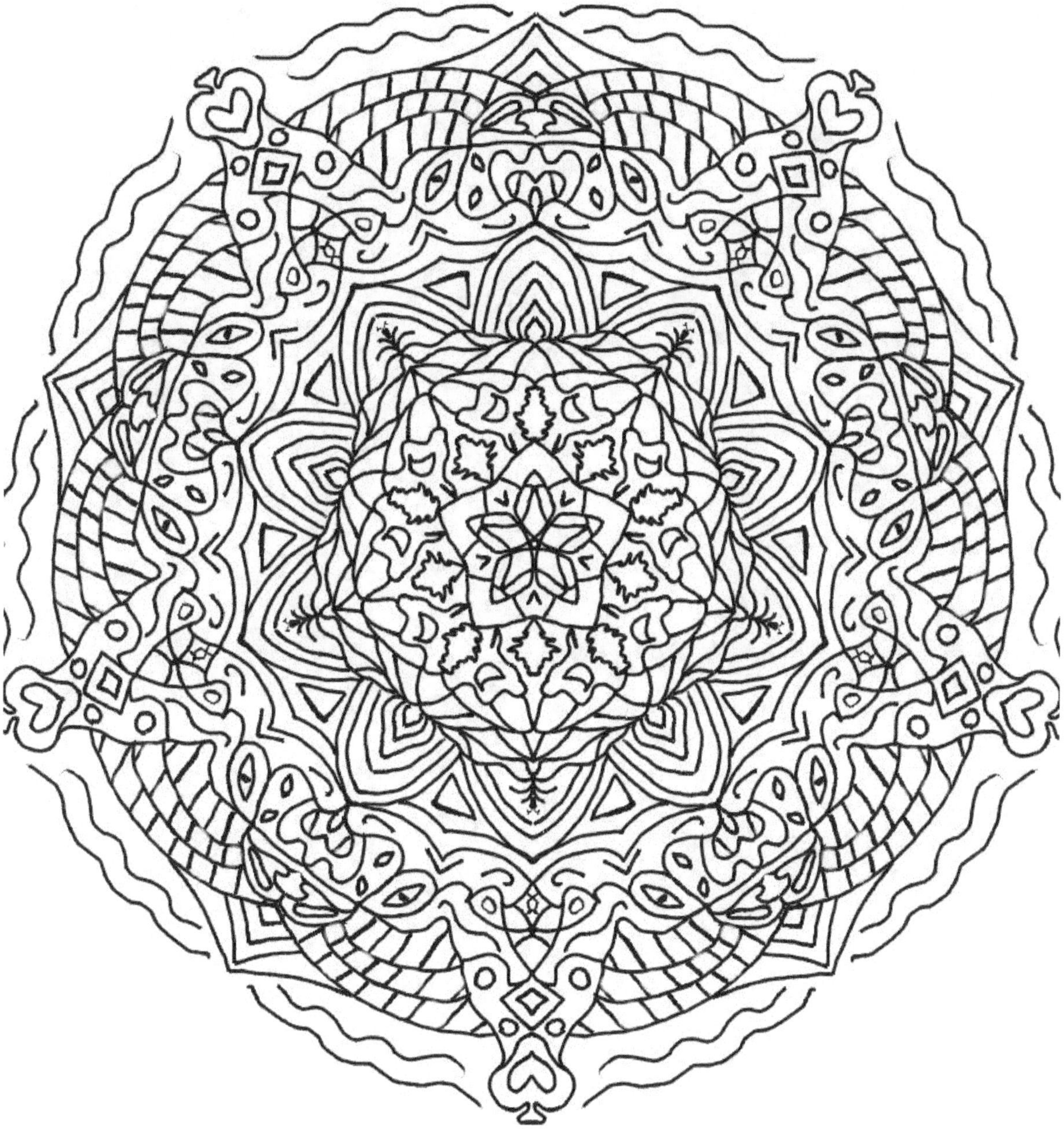

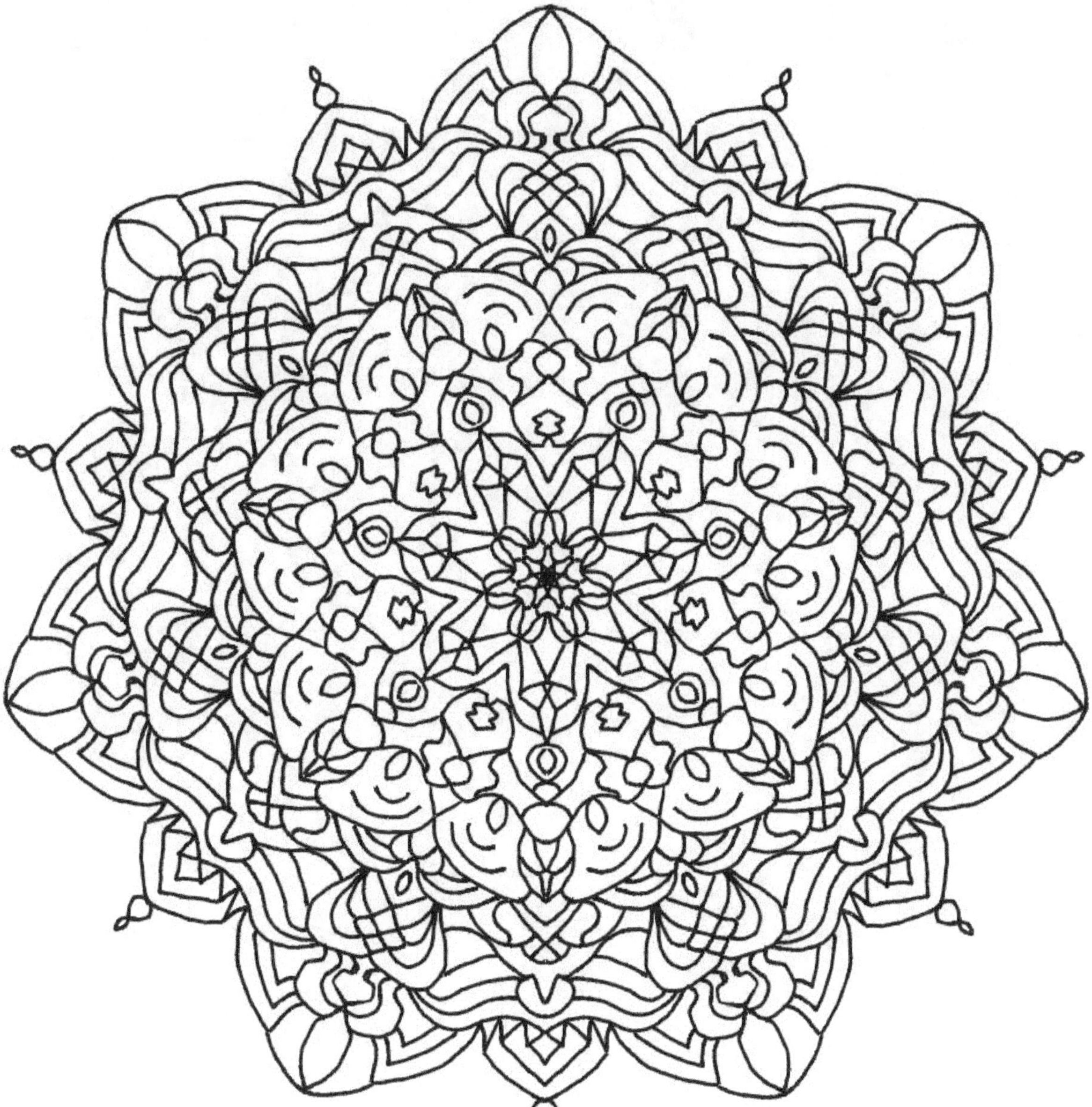

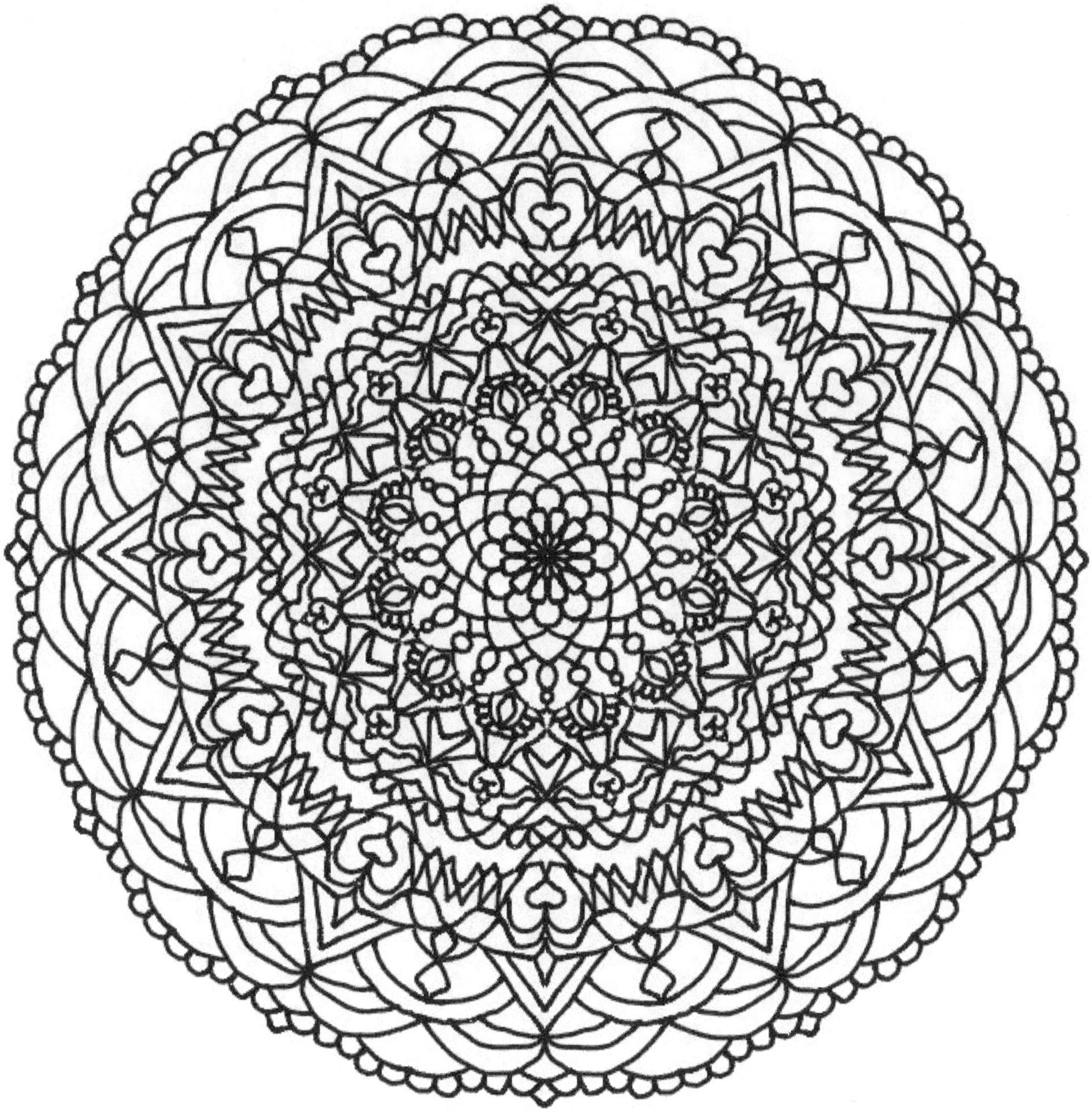

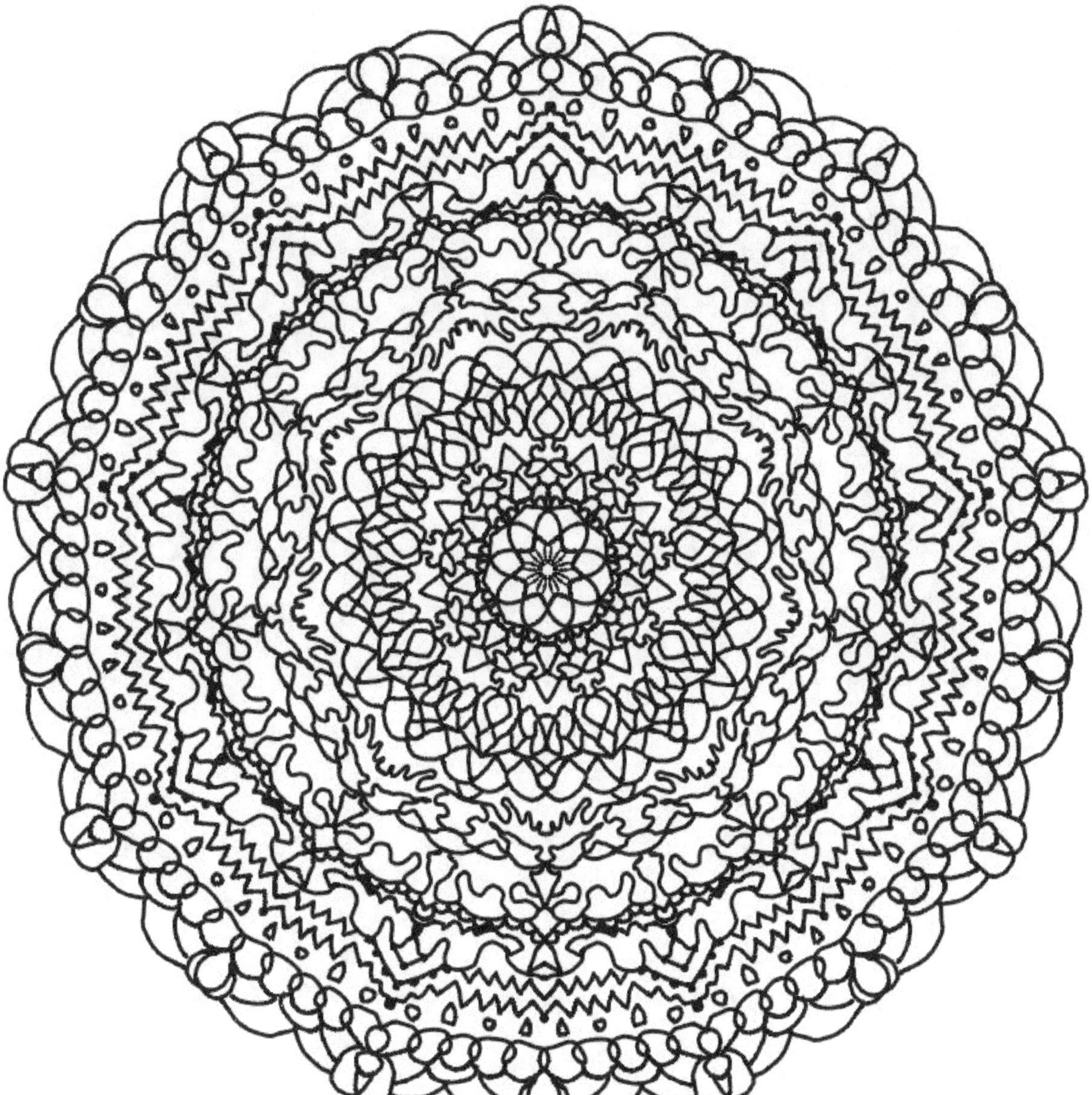

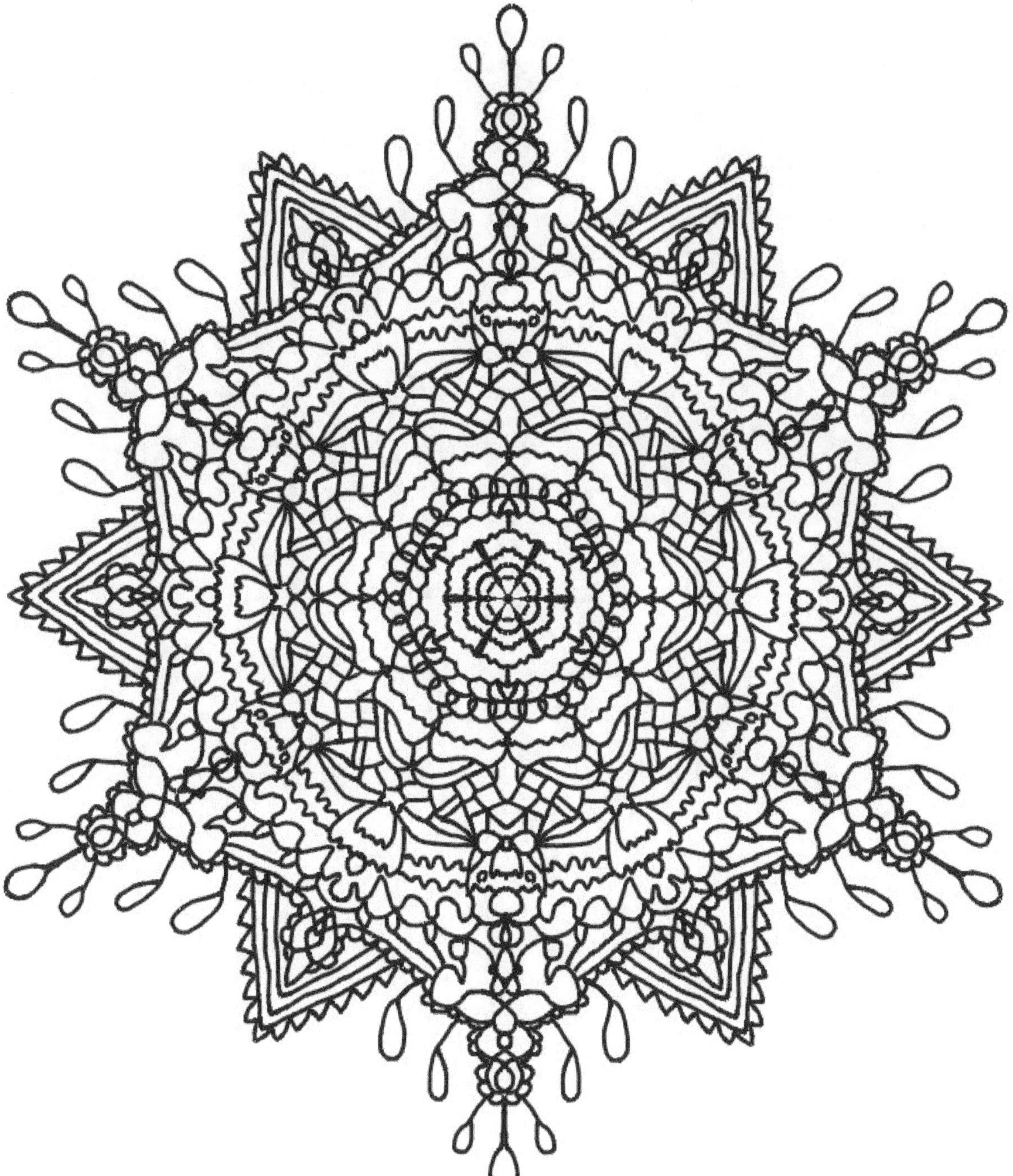

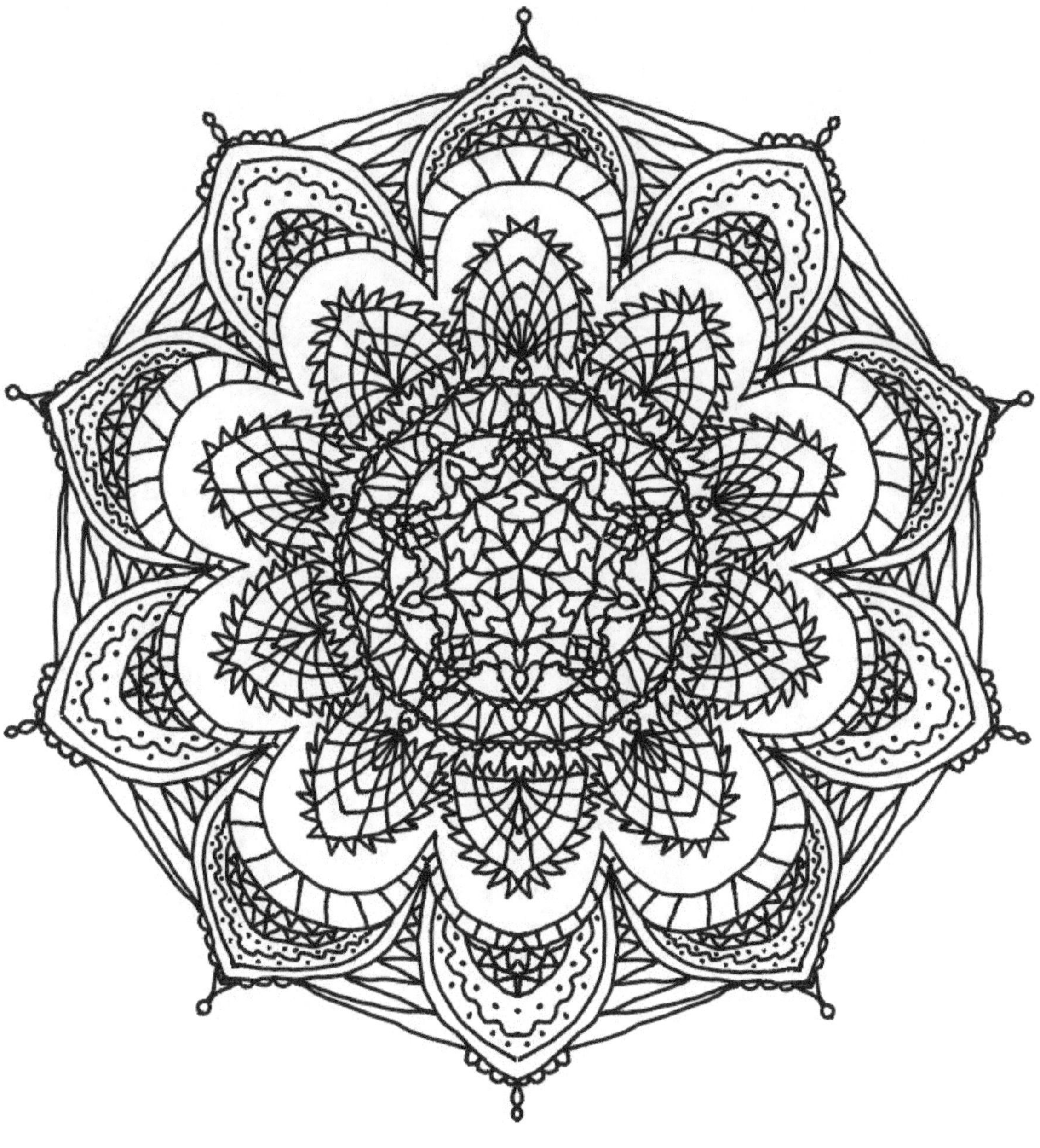

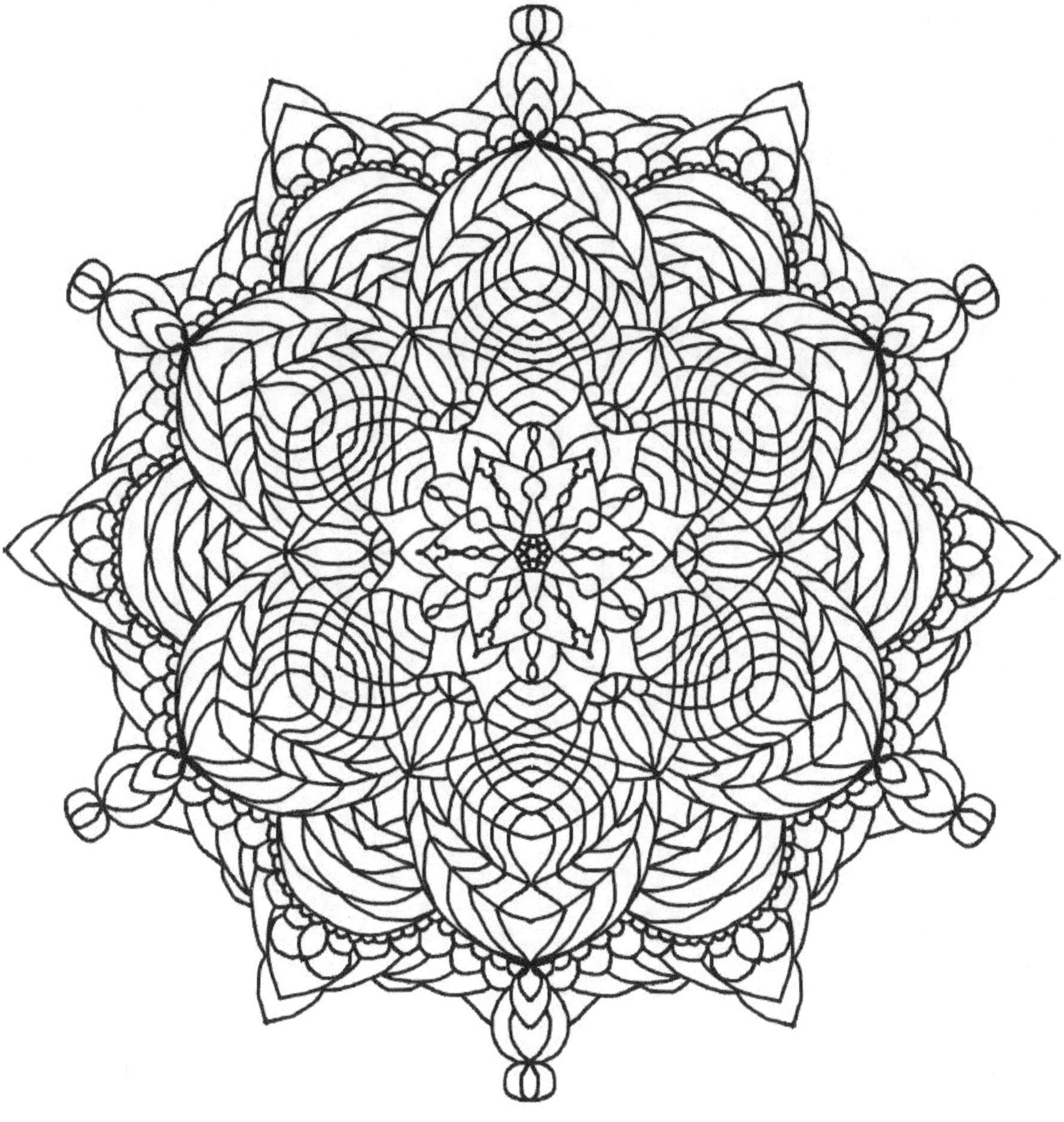

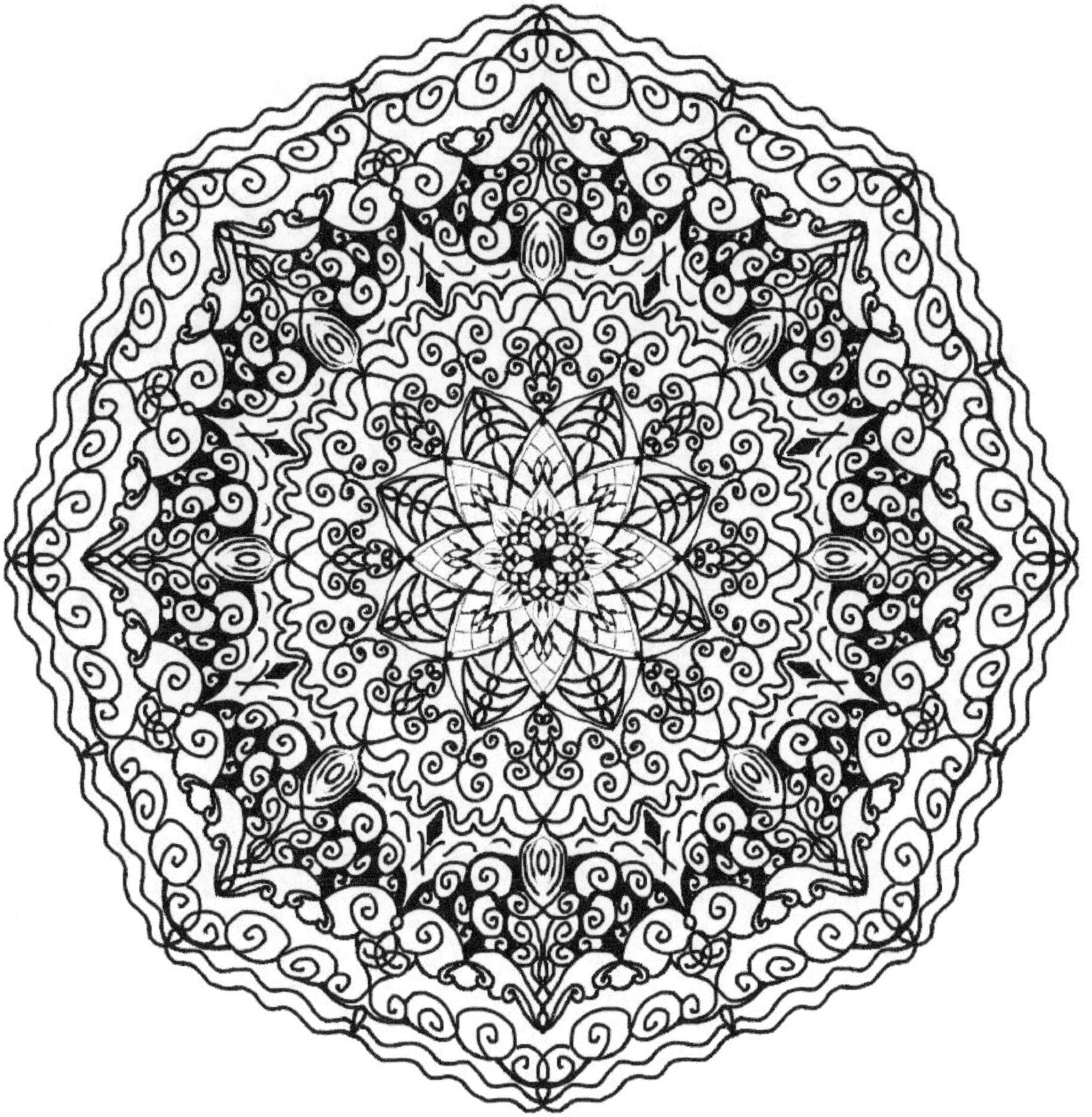

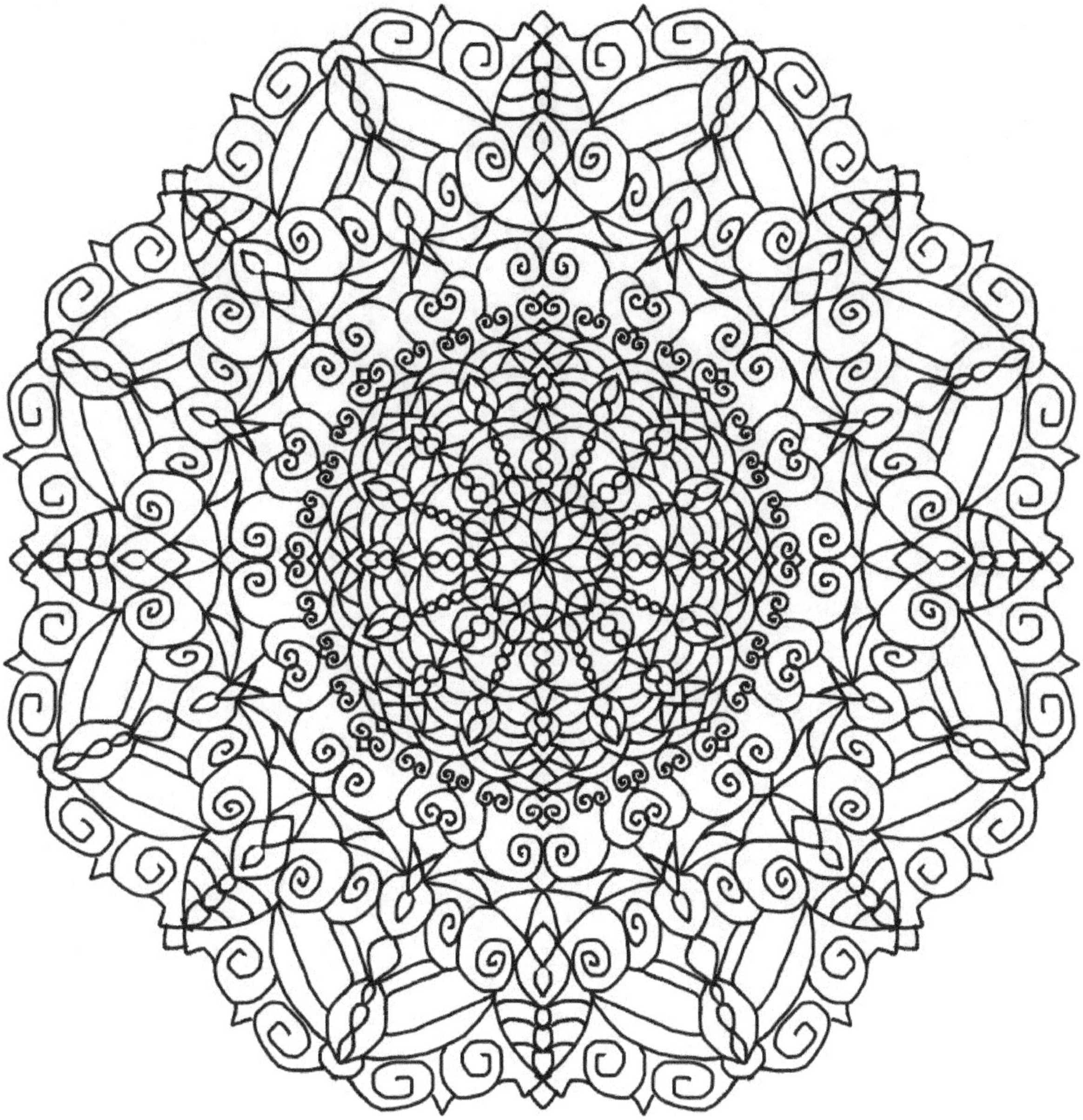

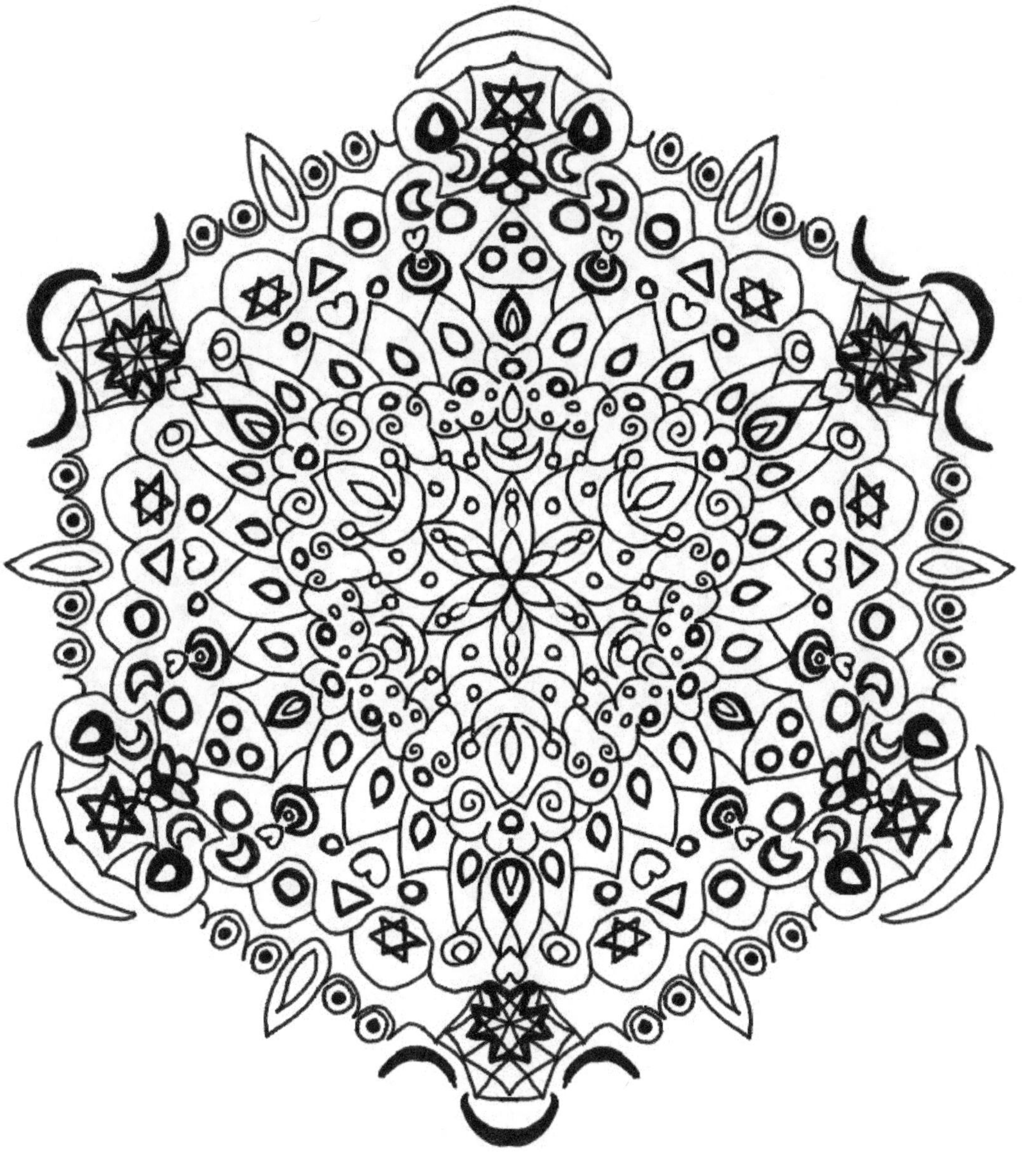

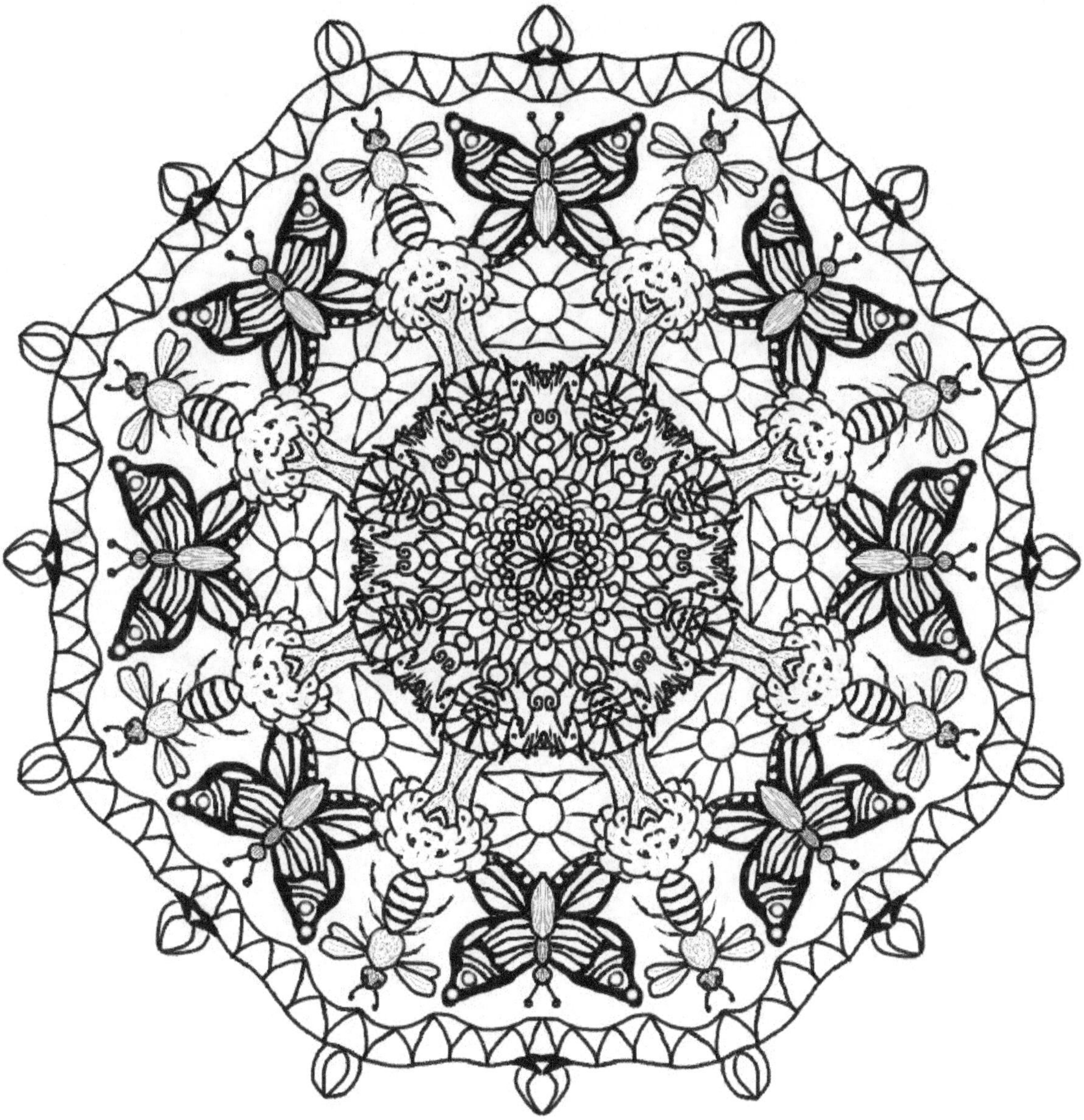

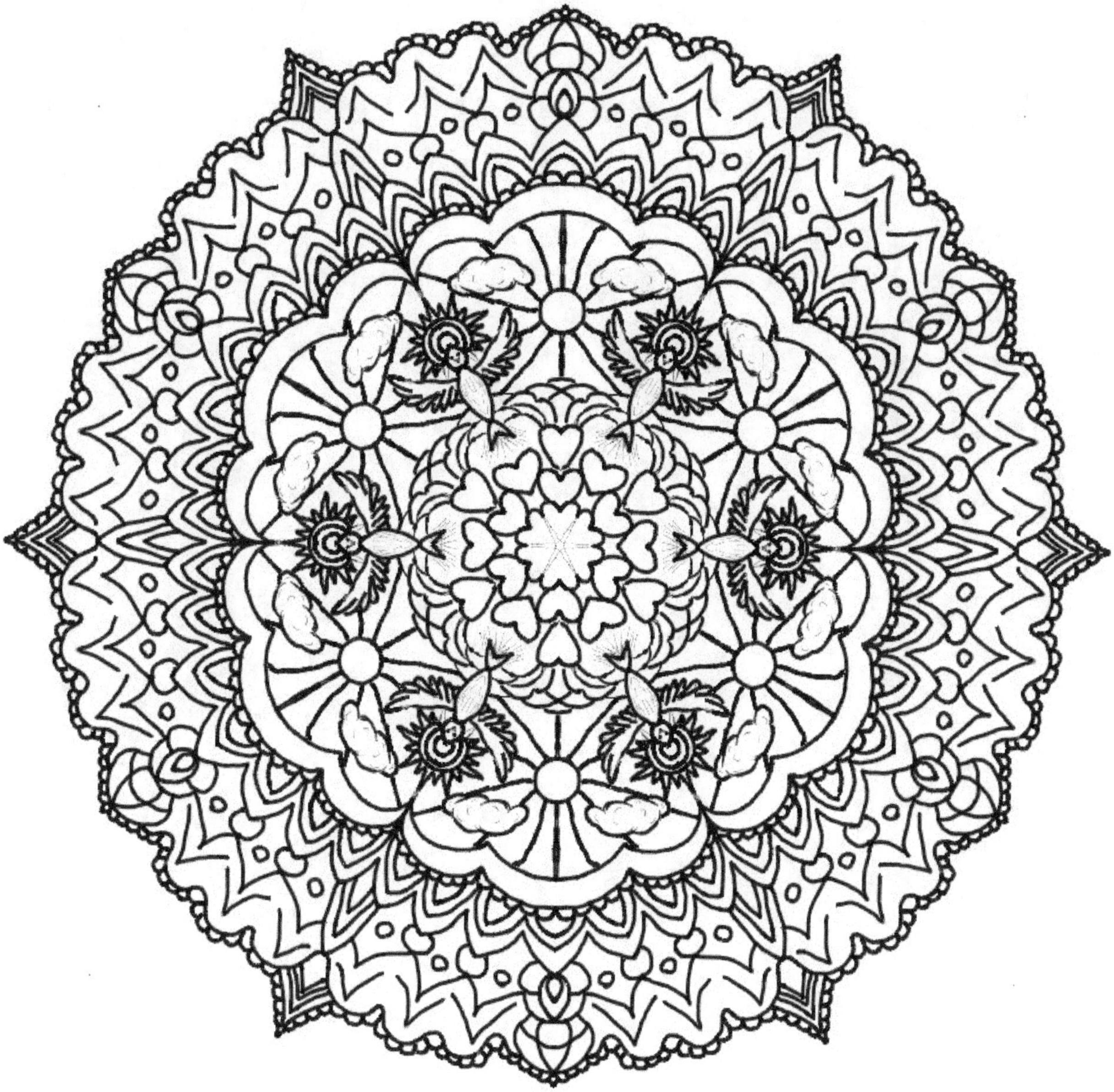

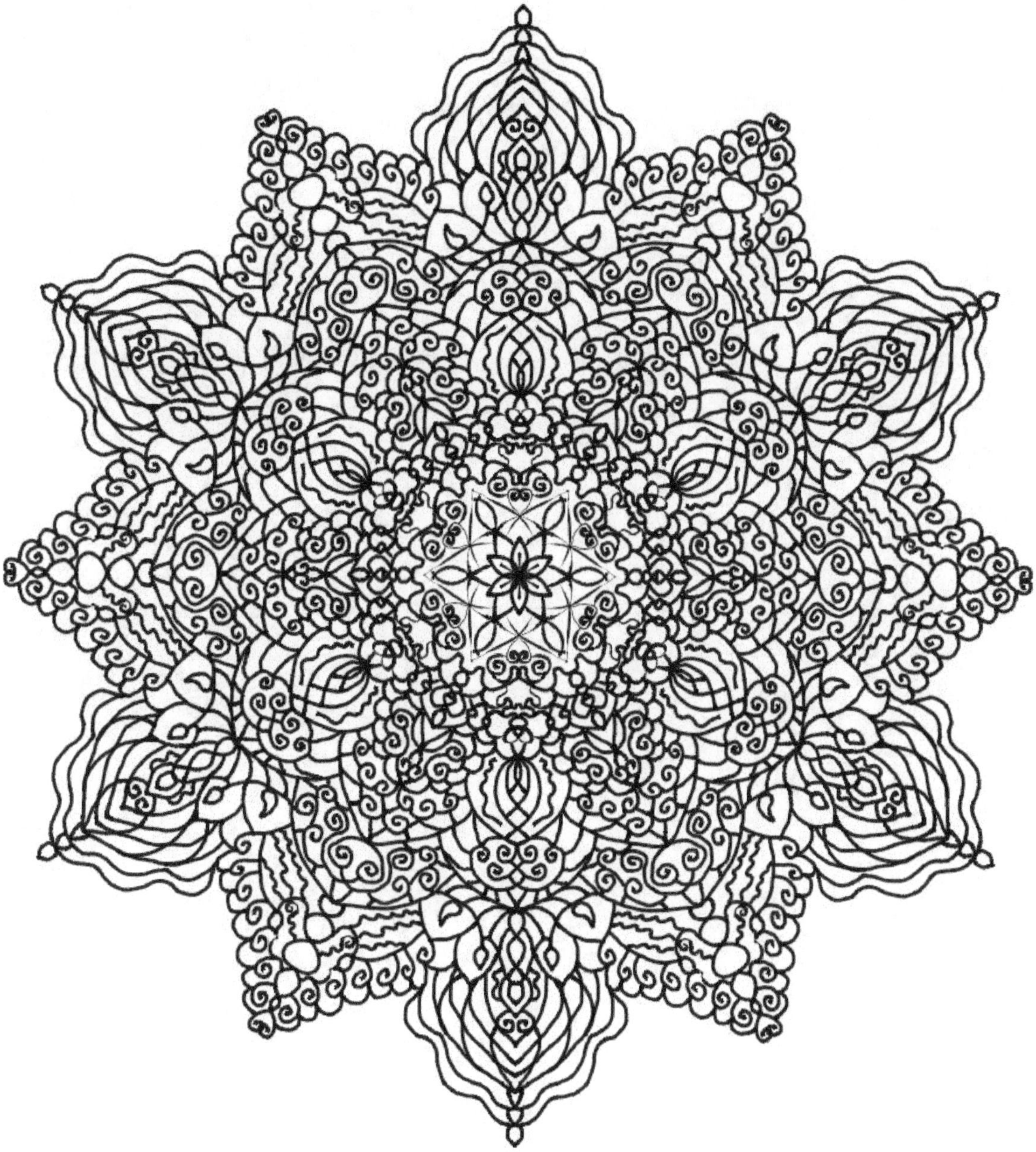

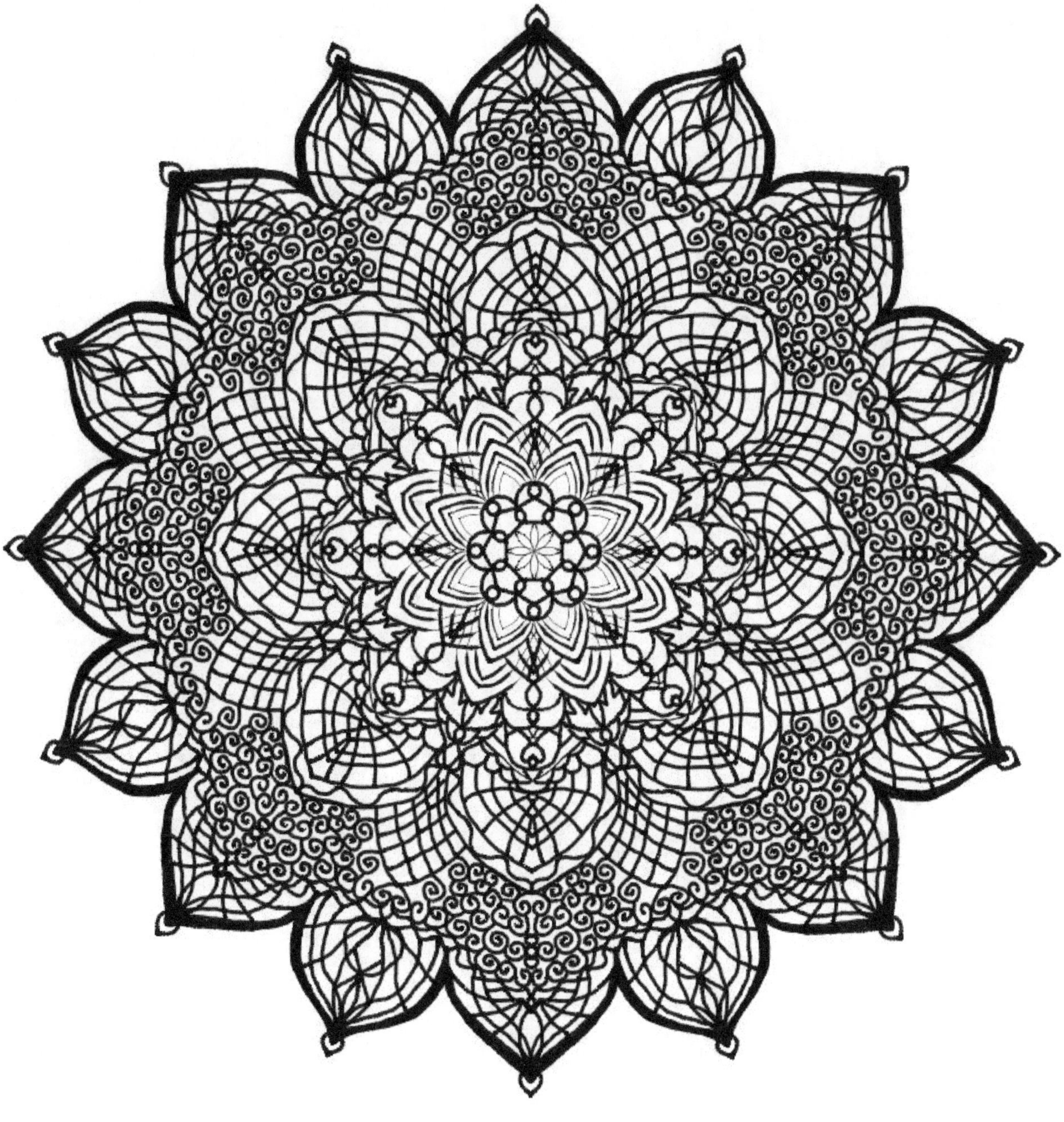

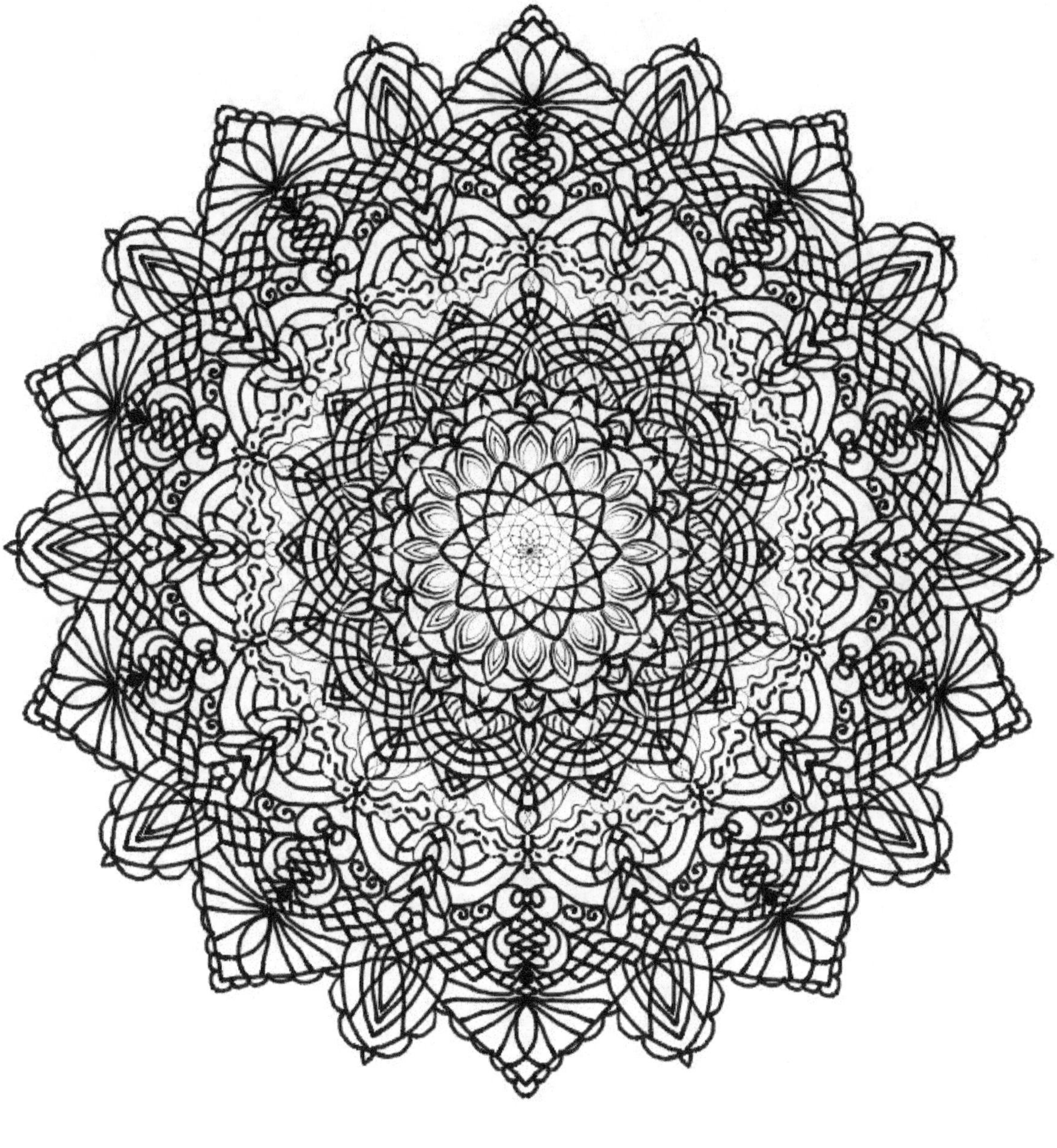

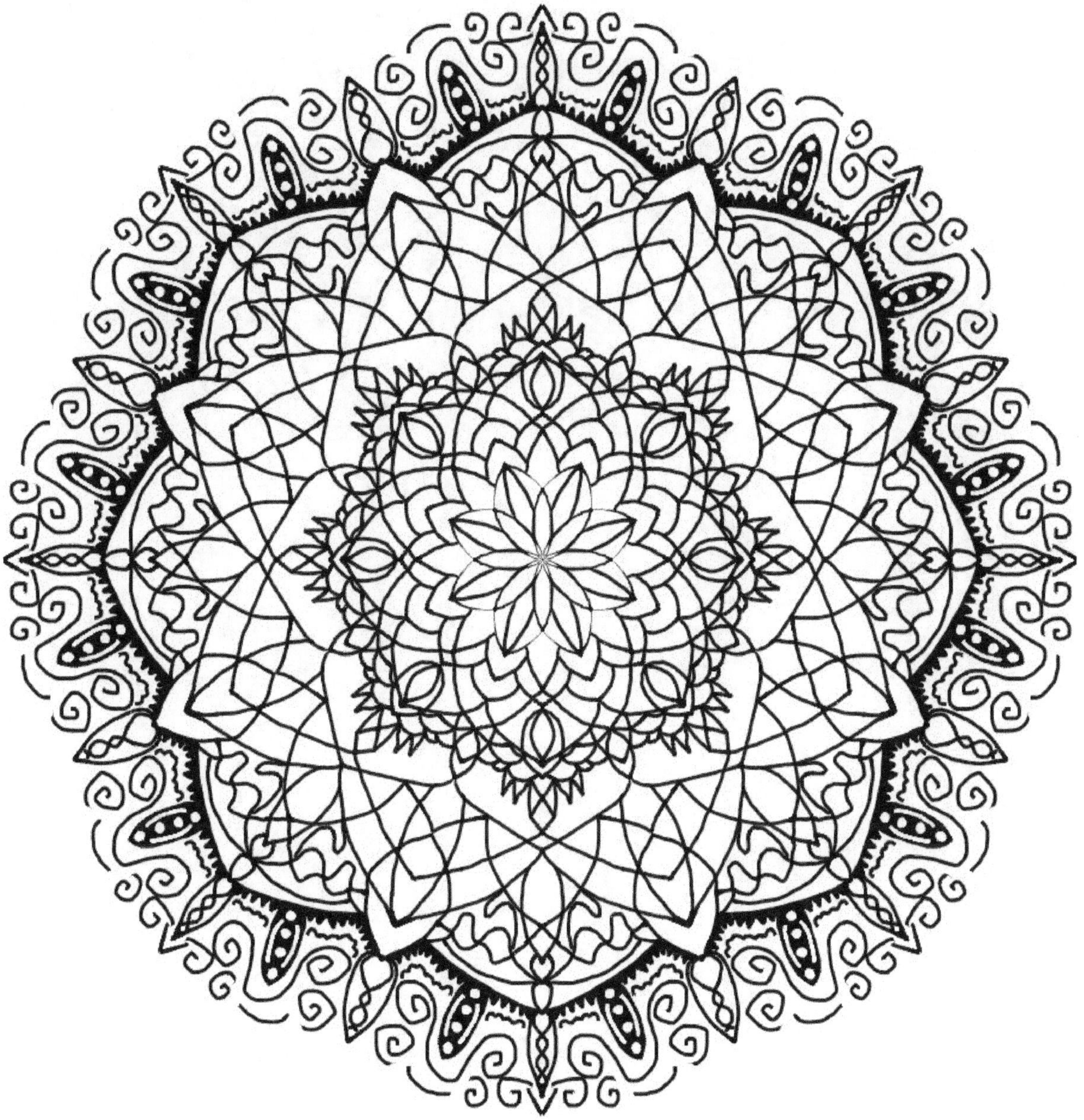

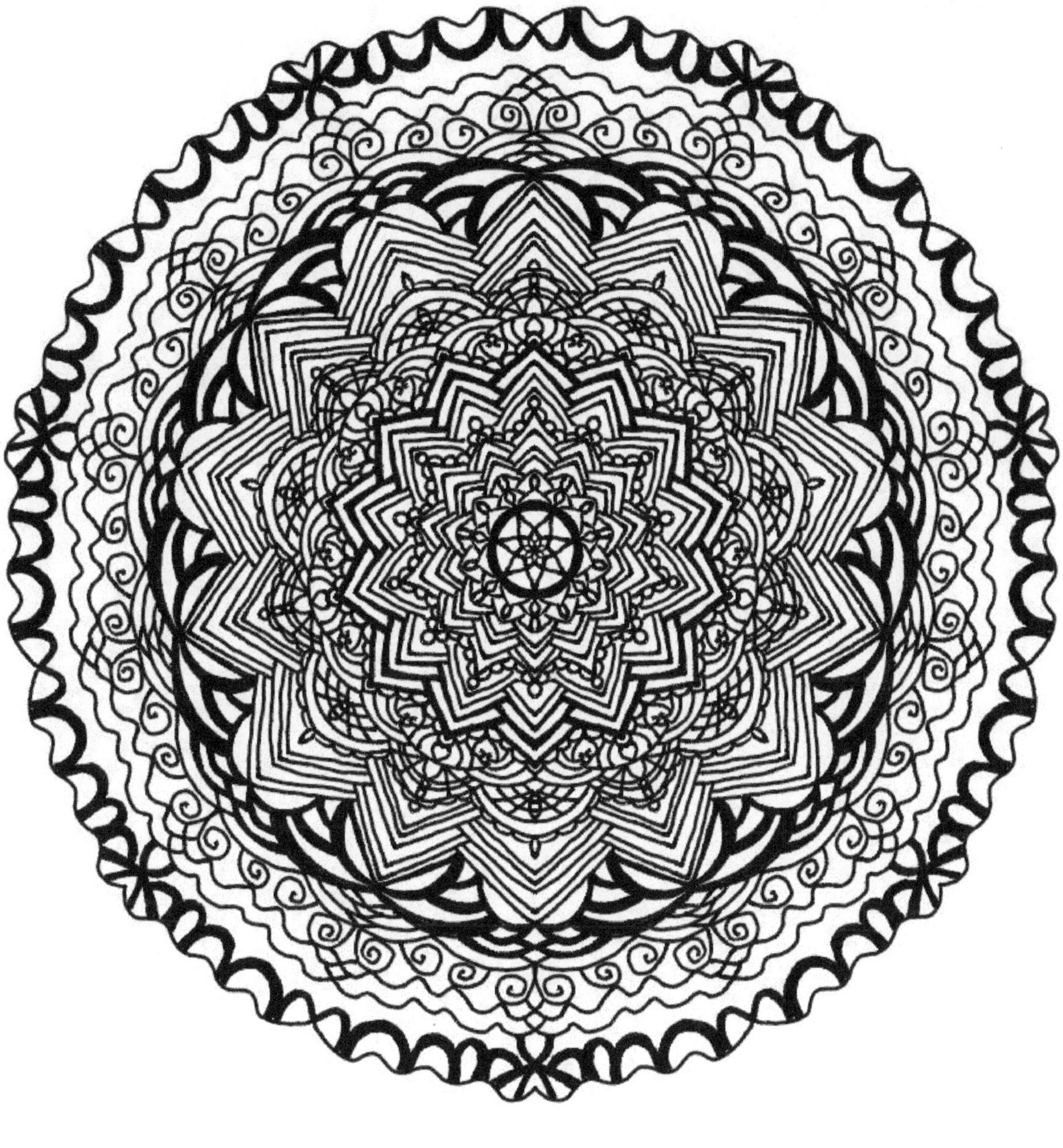

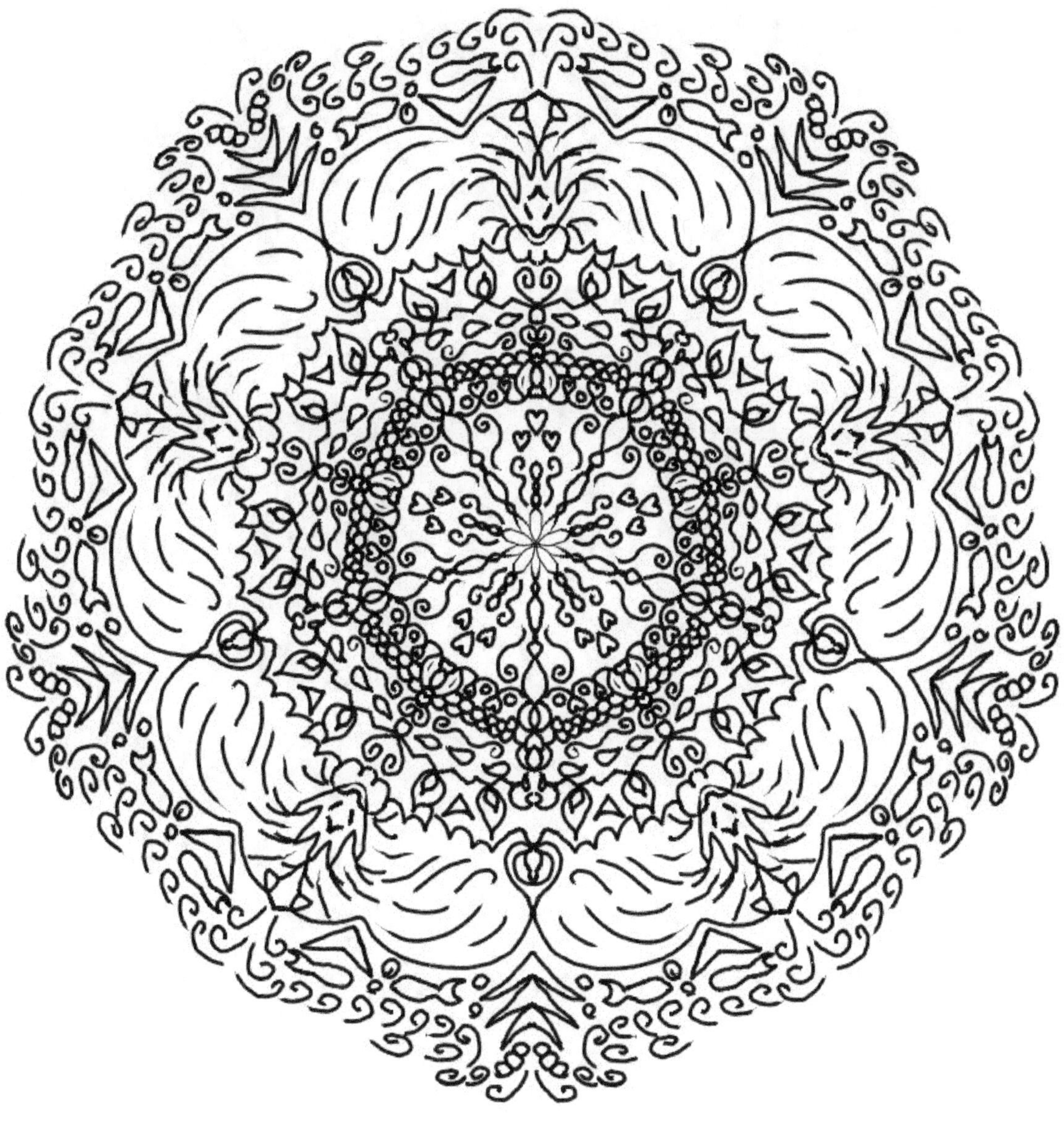

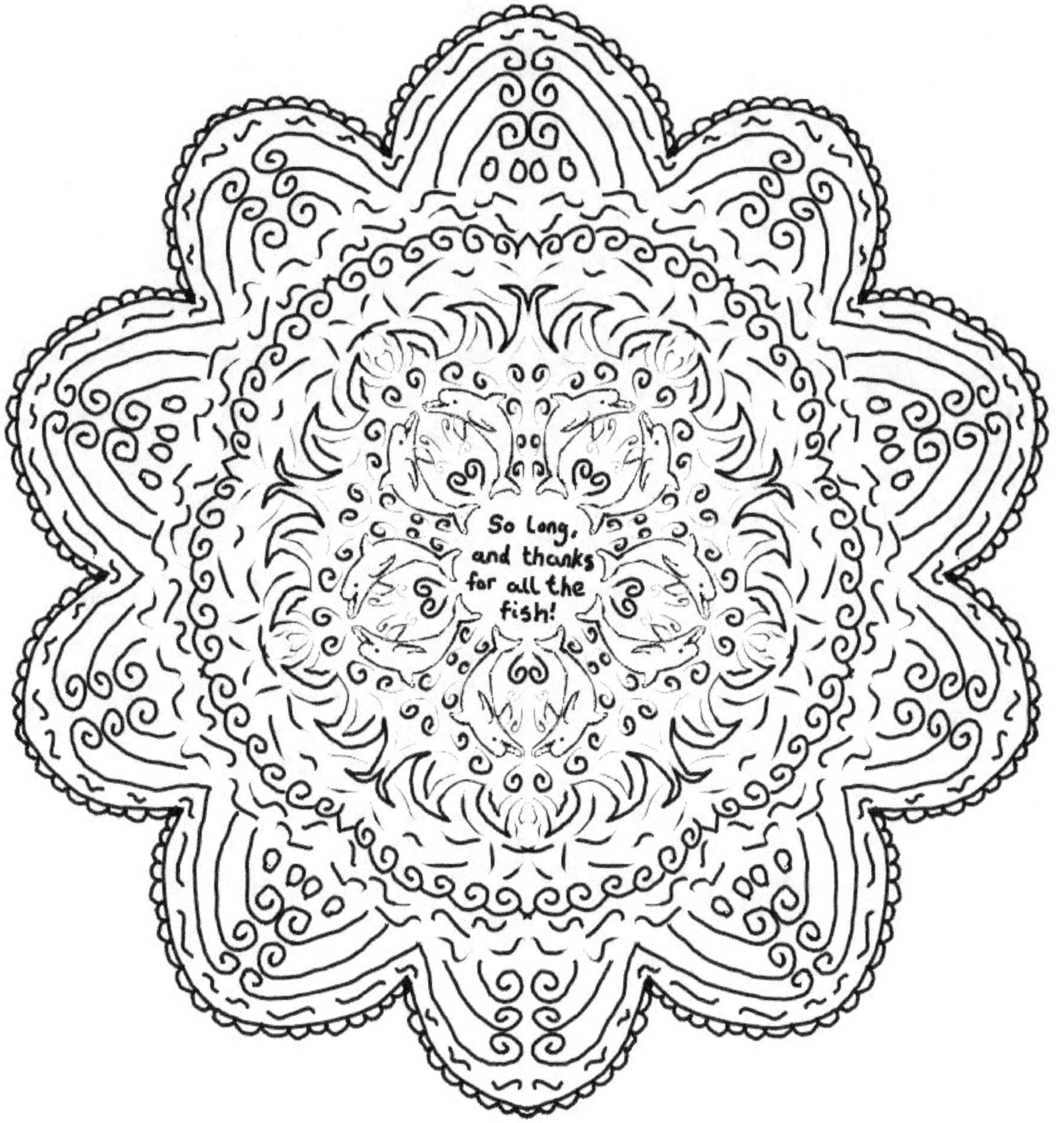
So long,
and thanks
for all the
fish!

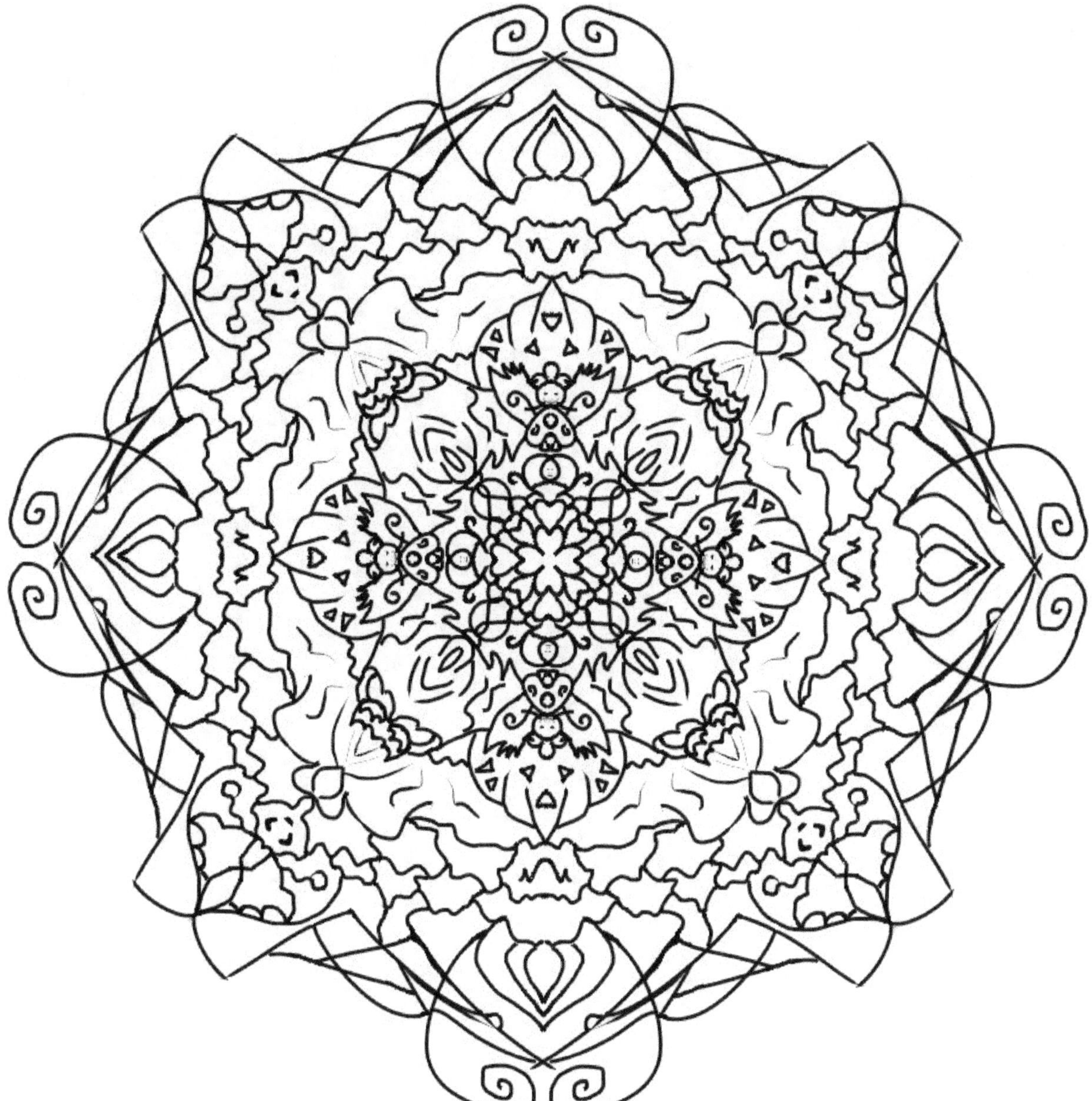

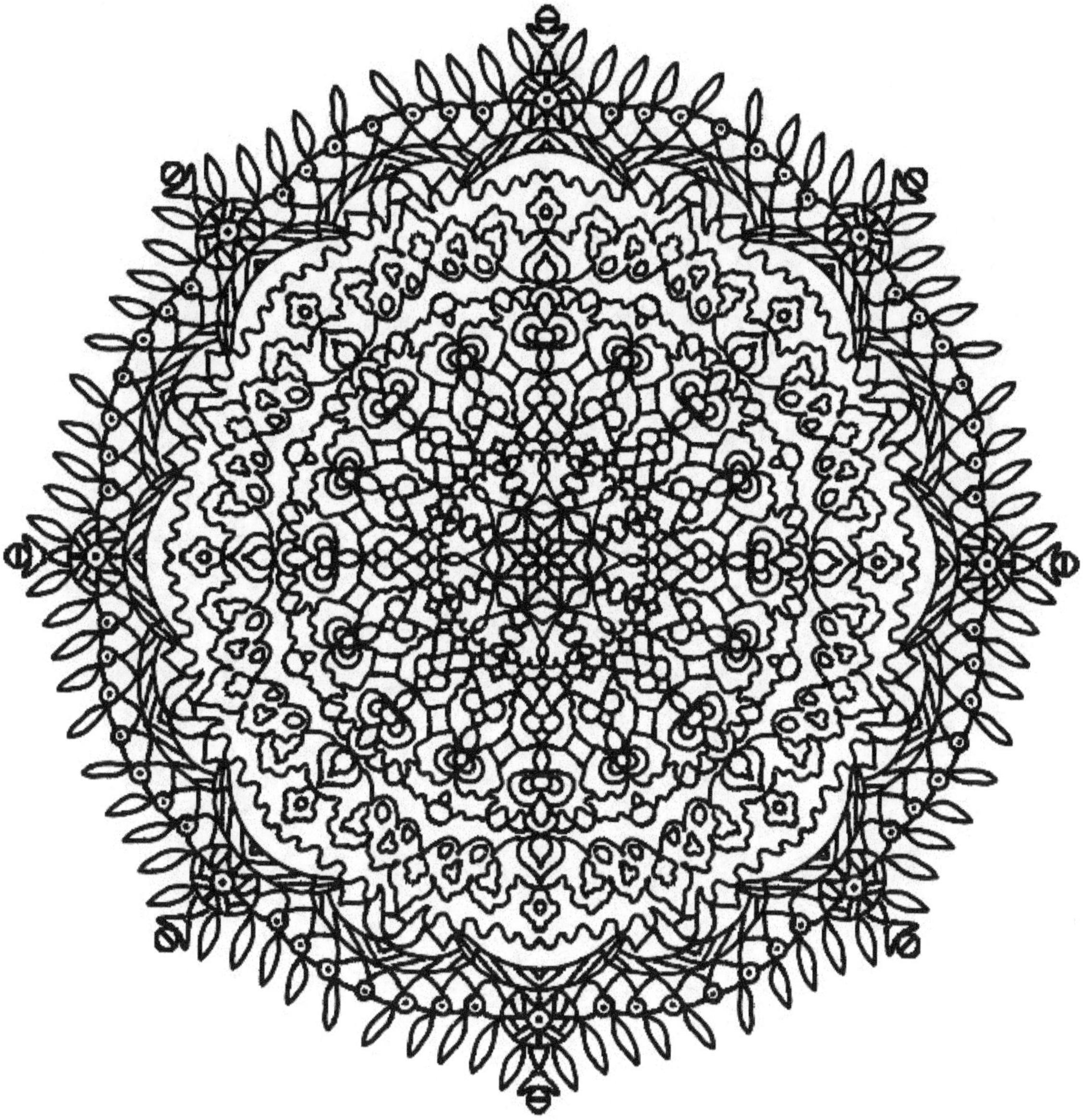

www.ingramcontent.com/pod-product-compliance
Lightning Source LLC
Chambersburg PA
CBHW080540190526
45169CB00007B/2573